About My

Father's Business

A 21st Century Psalmist

Garnet Earl Edwards, Jr.

authorHOUSE®

AuthorHouse™
1663 Liberty Drive
Bloomington, IN 47403
www.authorhouse.com
Phone: 1-800-839-8640

Published by AuthorHouse 5/10/2013

ISBN: 978-1-4817-3513-1 (sc)
ISBN: 978-1-4817-3514-8 (e)

Library of Congress Control Number: 2013905939

Dedication

To all those that I love and all who believe in me.

Psalm 1:3 (Amplified Bible)

[3]And he shall be like a tree firmly planted [and tended] by the streams of water, ready to bring forth its fruit in its season; its leaf also shall not fade *or* wither; and everything he does shall prosper [and come to maturity].

Table of Contents

About the Author

Deacon Garnet Earl Edwards, Jr., known as the "G-Man" and "Mack" to many, earned his Bachelor of Science Degree from West Virginia University in Morgantown, West Virginia in 1984.

After graduating from Welch High School in the mid-seventies, though he earned a football scholarship to attend West Virginia University, he was recognized by Stanley Romanoski, West Virginia University's track coach, as one of the premier track stars coming out of high school as a track All-American and Hall of Fame standout. After talking with the football scout, Paul Moran, it was agreed that Garnet would participate in his first spring football training camp in his freshman year and in the following years, would participate solely in the track meets through the University. He soon became an outdoor and indoor track sensation for the Mountaineers track team. In 1978 and 1979, he became Track Athlete of the Year for the State of West Virginia.

After setting records in several events for the Mountaineers track team, he was nominated to the All-American track team in 1979. Garnet's performance on the track field led him to All-American status as well as his induction into the West Virginia University's Sports Hall of Fame in 2001.

Playing football and running track at WVU, along with receiving his Bachelor of Science degree, opened many doors for Garnet.

Since that time, Deacon Edwards has spent the past 23 years caring for his parents. With the presence of his daughters Leah and Sarah and his wife Julia, the fullness of his life has unfolded. After his call to the ministry in 2008, his devotion to God has become his life's work to serve and obey.

He is a member and the Vice President of the Community of Praise Choir, McDowell County, WV under the direction of Sister Michelle Hargrave. In May 2012, Mr. Edwards was inducted into his hometown's Sports Hall of Fame in McDowell County, West Virginia.

A humble yet determined man, he attributes his success to God and to his loving family.

About the Book

A year ago, I was blessed to publish my first book of poems, "About My Father's Business." It was so well-received, and many encouraged me to continue my writing.

This 2nd edition of "About My Father's Business" contains the writings of a "21st Century Psalmist," so called because the words speak to the heart's fullness, of the trials and of the discontent of everyday life, as well as the deeply rooted spiritual concerns of one's soul.

It is intended to stir up your emotions. If you find these words strong, or hurtful, or joyful, or sad, then you are feeling what I am feeling. I know I have found solace in this 21st Century writing.

A Heart of Praise

When praises go up, blessings come down, and the spirit of the Lord, is felt all around
He's in the light and He's in the dark, and He moves throughout everybody's heart

So clap your hands, get up on your feet, trust in the Lord, because His word will keep

He's the Prince of Princes, He's the King of Kings
He is Jesus Christ, He's our everything

He's not the pain that we feel, or the heartbreak of sorrow,
But He is hope in our lives, for a better tomorrow

He is the bread of Life, our beginning and end
He is the love that we get, when we need a friend

He's Alpha and Omega, He's night and day
He's eternal life, when we have lost our way

So we praise Him in the morning, and in the darkest of night
We praise Him with a heart, that we know will magnify His light

A Little Peace of Heaven

A little peace of Heaven, is all that I need, and time has surely shown
me, in God I will succeed
The sum of my troubles, started with my heart, but truth as God knew
it, has never sold me short

I know that I am rich, and it is not measured by the standards of man

Way before I ever existed, God mapped out His plan

Some things that you will hear, I will not always explain
But I am lifted up to glory, that always acknowledges my name

So often we are faced, with life's hidden stories
So often we lose our peace of mind
I can tell you how to find that peace, God said, "Trouble, get thee
behind."

A little peace of Heaven, is all that we need
Because in His anointed, He has already planted His seed

Our steps are ordered, His word is sound
A little peace of Heaven, will never keep a good man down

Silence your fears, and return to the One
That will give you back your life, if you want to be reborn

That little peace of Heaven, is all that you need
Are you rich in His glory, do you believe?

A Walk in Spirit and Truth

We know our ancestors loved God, way before they became a slave
And their hearts carried that feeling, all the way to their graves

Like the Hebrews, that crossed over into the Promised Land
God did not forsake them, they too carried the burden of man

God created all men in His image, God treated them as a whole
The black man was enslaved, but it was his faith that saved his soul

Generations have come, and generations of people are gone
The black man did not perish, because the foundation of his faith was
strong

Some of us live our lives for the moment, but that time drifts away
Our hearts are feeble and cold, and the love in it won't stay

We are rich in tradition, we are bold, with no regrets
We follow God's law because, the truth doesn't let us forget

Do you want to be happy? Do you want to feel loved?
Then get off that ego trip and praise Him from above

Christians live above their senses, Christians live for eternal life
With God in their hearts, the world can't give them misguided advice

There are no more chains to be broken, there are no more chains to hold
us down
Jim Crow and Uncle Tom are lurking, but God's Word will keep them
bound

God has provided a way, for us to walk in spirit and truth
A lot of us have learned, but we have to keep teaching this to our youth

All Mothers Are Blessings

Mama, I can't begin to imagine, the things you've sacrificed
But I know that every Mom in this world, has somehow paid a price

I can't imagine, mama, what all it took
For you to write the first chapter, then someone comes along and closes
the book

I thank God for those mamas that stayed by our side
Even after the little girl dreams in them had died

Precious, is how mamas make us feel
Still some of us, will never know, that their emptiness is real

They protected us from the beginning with their heart of gold
They prayed for us over and over for God to bless our soul

They made us what we are today
We must continue to show them that our love is not drifting away

Precious, is how they make us feel
I pray in my heart that my mama's pain is healed
Because what she has taught me, was in Christ and truth, be still

Having a relationship with my mother, and her having a relationship
with me
Has given me the understanding that we should both be down on our
knees

To the moms all over the world, wherever you are, you will always be
our shining stars

America Woke Up

This morning we woke up, and everything seemed the same, but after
the smoke had cleared, the world spoke volumes to His name
Some searched for answers, knowing that the gray spots would remain

But the true hearts of democracy, used their energy not to complain
Was this the dream for many, or for others was it déjà vu
One thing is for certain, America has not turned her back on you

He believed that the best for us, was still yet to come
And the race that He had run, it was a race that wasn't done

Out came the message, from near and wide
You have four more years to help her
With the American people by your side
Some of course won't agree, but there has been a change
The America you once knew, is now mending back up her pain

This voice has been heard across the world, so let the truth be told
We are still America, and the Lord shall bless her soul

America: You Are Beautiful

There can be many ups, and way too many downs, but it takes
A pure heart to find peace that is sound
It takes a strong will to grow in life, but it doesn't take much to
fall, from the wrong advice

America you are beautiful, you are the country that I love
The pessimist tried to show me something different,
But God said, to keep my focus on the things above
The world said that they could give me silver, and fill my pockets with
gold
But God said that I wouldn't have His perfect love, that brings life
To my spirit and my soul

Letting the world go, He said, that I could have eternal life, because His
son Jesus, paid the price
He said that I could have, the desires of my heart if I believed, and I
Wouldn't come up short
America you amaze me with your red, white, and blue, you
Show us your true colors
But some, make a mockery out of you

Your heart is sound and your people are strong
We will always succeed America, because you are still our Home

God is the pillar that keeps it all real, whatever differences
We've had, surely, they will heal

God is the Creator, of all men
Don't see me as your enemy, but see me, as your friend

Angry

We are not defined by tragedy, but how we carry on
We might be angry, but God's grace and mercy keep us strong
We will never forget, this tragedy that came our way
And the search for our resolve, will always be our mainstay
America is still number one in this world, and still number one in this land
Because her power is built on truth, and freedom for every man

As the world watched, the Twin Towers tumbled to the ground
We vowed that every terrorist, and their act would be found

We vowed to be united, and united to take a stand
We pray that we will never, ever see, nine-eleven again

Shanksville, PA, will never be the same
It was there that flight ninety-three, crashed in a field in flames
The forty innocent people that died, were heroes that day
And as a result of their brave act, a fifteen-hundred acre national park, covers the field where they lay
The Pentagon was also hit, killing one hundred and twenty-five
When that plane crashed down on that protected building, military and civilians died
Tell me al-Qaeda, the destructor of man, does God hold your life in the palm of His hand
America is still the beautiful, and she is still the land of the free
Angry we are, but don't misconstrue what you see
She's a better country, she stands firmly in the palm of God's hand
We were all made in God's image, but it is in His promise that we will stand

We won't give up, certainly won't give in
The world is changing, but we still know how to pick our friends
God said that it was okay to get angry
But He said not to sin
We are not defined by our tragedies, but how we finish in the end

Another One Of Those Mornings

How can the lost, be so lost, how can the blind, not have eyes to see

This is another one of those mornings, when things have finally gotten the best of me

I live in this small community, right out side of town
I am peaceful, I am content, but being suddenly woken stirs my peace around

Some of those noises, so far away but clear, how can I be hearing them, when I abide down here

The rudeness of some people in this community, who just don't care
They never worry about their effects on others,
Not even the elderly whose hearing is fair

Lord please forgive me for my worry, and forgive them for their lack of concern
You told me to trust you, because we are all going to learn
It's not about me, but yes I hear you Lord
I am on Calvary's hill, looking for my reward

Another one of those mornings, but it's going to be okay
I live in a small community, and Heaven is not far away

Are We Finishers

I was asked this question once, and now I can reply
I can only clear the speck, that exists in my own eye

I have been a student, throughout most of my life
Searching for answers, looking for Christ

And after I realized, that I too held the key
The spirit of Jesus, fell down on me

I am God-approved, and I come from the dust
The road that I have traveled, was one in spirit but consumed in lust

We have all gone down this road before
But there was Jesus who can close that door

Knowing that we are all finishers,
We have a story to tell, even if the story doesn't turn out well
To the young and to the old, the Lord our Jesus can save our soul

Be In It, To Win It

Life is never fair, you might find some that care, still dream if you dare,
but you'd better be aware
Be in it, to win it, that's all

Time does bring about a change, among other things
But we must know who we are, as we follow that shining star
Be in it, to win it, that's all

I am what I am, this, I know now
You can't, get me down, because His love and peace is sound
I'm in it, to win it, that's all

You and I, both know, that it is our heart
That the world tries to steal, there are times we give it at will
But it is not the world's, it is yours and mine
We're in it, to win it, that's all

We have learned our lessons well
When it counted, we have excelled
And how we made it through, with what we had to do
We were in it, to win it, that's all

We are the same, we believe in Jesus' name
In Him there is no shame, in truth there is no blame
He's in it, to win it, that's all

Be Still

You might hear it in a whisper, you might feel it in a touch
But it will be still enough, for you to experience the rush

So listen, listen, listen, listen, it will come, Christ the Savior the Son
And no other voice will be sweeter heard, than the one
No other voice, will bid you to come

I have been converted, I am truly convinced
Beyond the shadow of a doubt, I've been Heaven sent

Within my spirit, and deep in my soul
God is, I am, that is all you need to know

Being Instructed, Now

I had looked outside for instruction, all of my life
When I had been taught, that my anchor, was always Jesus Christ
I had been fearful, way too long, listening to hear His call, trying to shut
down what I thought was wrong
I knew from my childhood, that His word was real
And I knew my destiny would lead me, where my peace would be still
But as I grew older, I let fear and the world get me down
Instead of looking on the inside, being happy for what was found
In the word of God, there is nothing new, the voice of the Lord, has
finally broken through
I am in this life, what God says I am
The Son of a King who will never back down
I am that light that shines up on a hill
I am the strength of my brother, when he has lost his will
Satan is a liar, God will always have our back
He is peace and comfort, wherever we are at
As subtle and naive that the devil tries to be
He has nothing to do with you, and nothing to do with me
In the mighty name of Jesus, we are instructed to teach His word
And to preach when called, when the discipleship is heard

Blinded By The Light

I want to believe, that everybody knows about the power of God
I want to believe, that once you experience His power
Nothing else in your life, will ever be robbed
I want to see change in that burglar, who tries to break in and steal
I want to see change in that atheist, who doesn't believe that God is real

There is only, but one power, and God stands alone
He is the Prince of Peace, He is our King of Kings, on the throne
When you are blinded, by His light, He will heal your mind, touch your
body, and give you back your sight

The enemy has taken many victims, it has destroyed
Individual, and family lives
It comes when we least expect it, but in God's house, the enemy is
nothing but lies

God is there for our pain, and He is there for our sorrow
Jesus came along, to show us that there is a better tomorrow
We are beautifully and wonderfully made, Jesus died at that cross
So our debt is paid
Rise up, from that doubt and your fears, the God of creation, will wipe
away your tears

Bluefield's Early Morning

Red light, green light
Flags blowing in the wind
Men working across the way
Trying to get a full day in

Trucks, cars, going by
Steam from a nearby building
Dissipating in the sky

The Greyhound bus passing on time
Stopping at sites along the line
As the town awakens,
This early morning day
The fog clears….
To a lighter shade of gray

As I cut my eyes to the left
I saw someone I knew
Looked like they had a hard night, my
What people put themselves through

This site on a hill
Is no longer still
Like a flower that awakens in the sun
That's what this little town has done

Red light, green light
The day carries on,
I'm here now
But soon I'll be gone.

Born Blessed

It didn't take long afterwards, for me to understand the rest
When I had found out at an early age, that I was born to be blessed

Sitting here on my front porch, admiring Your presence, and feeling
Your love
I'm so thankful that You had me in mind, when You poured out Your
blessings down from above

My consciousness rode high that day, because I knew that You were
there
I knew that You would hear me, O Lord, and I knew that You would
care

I honor You this day, O Lord, on my knees I pray
I pray for those who are lost, I pray that Your spirit will show them the
way

They were also born free, blessed above measures, that only their pure
hearts can see
Being born again in the body is a precious sight,
Thank you dear Lord, that I see the light

To be able to see, to be able to hear, to feel Your presence, that is always
so near,
I am blessed

Thank you, Lord, for loving me, and letting me be all, that I could be
Thank you for this freedom, that is resting comfortably and bold
It gives me the strength, to honor you with my soul

But most of all, Lord, thank you, that I was born blessed
In the presence of Jesus, my soul does rest

Born to Victory

God has always given us mercy, to stay in the race
The wiles of the devil will never steal our grace

The truth of life is possible, if we just believe
Let His Grace and His Mercy, keep us down on our knees

I once was lost, thank God I am found
I had the world weighing on my shoulders, which tried to keep me down

I looked up to the Father, who reminded me of His Son
He said to get up, because my work in this life is not done

Give your problems to Jesus, who rejoices in saving souls
He'll put you on the right track, right back up to Victory Road

If we can get past ugly, our little light will shine
Remembering where we come from, and believing victory is yours and
Mine

There will always be hope, when trouble is around
There will always be a Savior, who we can call on now

He is Alpha and Omega, our beginning and our end
We were born in Victory, but still we have to fight sin

Let God's mercy and His grace always keep us sound
Let the love that is in our lives, keep us well and never down

We are going to have problems, but they exist there to let us know
That God will never leave us
He will keep peace in our souls

Bound To The Promise

As I set here before my teacher, being as humble as I can be
I know that I exist to encourage others, but will the old man die in me

My teacher's words were so inspiring, his commitments were strong I'm
encouraged to utter them out in life, because my passion for the truth
must live on

I can prepare myself by the things that He says, and be careful at the
things that I do, because my brother, in this world, I have much love for
you
Knowing that the God head, dwells inside of me, His bountiful
blessings, are what I want to see

Many words have been spoken, life brings about so many trials
But the one thing that really counts in my heart, is that I know that I
am God's child

The teacher's words were comforting, as he shepherded me as his friend
He doesn't want me to be frustrated, but he wants me to answer my call
as it begins

I know that with his help, and with the blessings from the Lord
I will come to understand, that eternal life, is my reward

There will always, be ways, for God's light to shine in
Simply by staying on my knees, God's love will protect me from the
devil in men

Bound to the promise, for a truth that I know is real
Is everything that I believe in, especially the way that God's love makes
me feel

Brave Hearted

You have endured, so much pain
But you came through it, in Jesus' name
You took the road, to a brand new life
Now you are holding hands, with Jesus Christ

You are the miracle, that didn't get away
God saw it in your heart and said, that you would be okay
He made you strong, and He made your enemies weak
He saw Satan fall, right beneath His feet

This is the way, that it is supposed to be
God planted the seed, then He harvested the fruit, from that tree
You chose to accept it, that life that you have left
You may seem alone, but I tell you, that you are not, by yourself

God is your refuge, your strength, and the light
He is the truth, that makes everything alright
I am a witness, because He made me whole
Something in me was missing, then He touched my spirit and saved my
soul

Jesus is the light, for the whole world to see
They have been blinded, but your brave heart has been set free

Burning On An Endless Wave

A bomb goes off, inside my head
Boom, those thoughts are dead

Bomb's gone, burning on an endless wave
Resting peacefully, in its grave

Allowing time, to reach its own
With not one whisper, that it's gone

Bam, look at me now
You crushed my heart, 'til you got it down

You pulled my thinking to the ground
It was God who blessed, the peace I found

So my time goes on
And your pitiful soul shall roam

Throughout, eternity
Lonely, looking up at me

Screaming, give me one more chance
But you played the song, to your last dance

You did it, you made the choice
Now you have, a silent voice

Resting miserably, in your grave
Burning on an endless wave

Celebrate And Rejoice

We are gathered in this place, because we have chosen to run this race
It is because of our loved ones, and our friends, and the stranger on the
street
It is in our hopes, and our prayers, it is what we want to beat

So we celebrate to remember, and fight to never forget, that the battle is
not with cancer
It is the thought of losing our loved ones, that we fret

I have known a lot of people, who have fought to the end
And they also realized that it was Jesus
Who fights the battles, of all Men

They committed themselves to the truth, because they knew that the
truth, would set them free
And the fear that they had, was not knowing
That in God, what would be, would be

I've known cancer survivors, and their hearts have always, touched my
soul
Their spirit has lifted me up, and their truth, much sweeter than gold

Celebrate to remember, and fight, to never forget
We will have trials, and tribulations, but the God of all creation, is not
through with us yet

Change Something

I want to believe, that everything is good, and that the
Big bad wolf, doesn't live in this neighborhood

I want to believe, that everybody is a friend, that I can
Love my neighbor, in spite of his sin

I want to believe, that my word is my bond, and when I
Have been wronged, I have the strength to forgive and press on

Because as many blessings as God provides, we should
All be doing more things, with our lives

You may be my relative, or you may be my friend, but a
Heart that is not focused, will still lose in the end

So should we live in hope, will we live in fear, do we
Have a comforter, will our eyes be filled with tears

I won't speak for you, but I know God for myself, the
Truth that I am trying to live, is for Him and no one else

There is a healer, and a happy end to this story, and it is
God, who fills us with His glory

I will pray but I also must believe, that if I change something,
My soul will be at peace

Christ Delivers

The storms came a-raging, right through our little town
The trees were blowing over, as they shattered to the ground

The winds were very strong, as the rain started falling hard
Debris was flying, it had caught us all off guard

I checked on my daddy, to see if he was doing okay
My little girl called last night, and said the storm was on its way
She said, that she was worried, because the news looked pretty bad, West
Virginia was in the path of that storm and she was worried about her
dad
I got down on my knees, I said the Lord's Prayer
I prayed for my little girl, who has such a big heart to care
Lord keep your arms around her, and let her know that You are there,
Tell her that she is blessed, and that she is the daughter of a King, and
your Son Jesus Christ, has her under His wings
Lord, bless our little town, through the billows that roll
Guide us one and all, and give peace to our soul

Community Of Praise

Hey out there, we're Community of Praise
It's time to get, our spirits raised

Clap your hands, and stomp your feet,
God and His word, cannot be beat

We're the choir of the hour, we're here to sing
We know that, praise and worship is everything

We sing in spirit, we bring hope alive
Those who believe, will not be denied

We believe that hope, is yours and mine
We believe that truth, is what you'll find

So clap your hands, and stomp your feet
The Community of Praise, is a choir that Jesus seeks

Confess And Rest

Speak with confidence, say what is on your mind
Never let the world tell you, that peace is not what you will find

Man was made in God's image, but man has gone astray
Speak with conviction, the truth in you will find its way

God said that every life was precious, He said that your time was now
Who else but Jesus, can keep you on solid ground

Shadrach and Meshach, and Abednego
Prayed night and day because, they believed that God would bless their
soul

The King didn't want to do it but he ordered his furnace hot
He put them in that fire and God comforted them on the spot
They had confessed in their spirit, then they let it rest
Then God took over, after the King had put their faith to the test
What am I saying, do not be deceived
Confess and worship, fall down on your knees and believe
You might be looking for answers, and you might not be sure of yourself
You have the mind of Jesus, and there can be nothing else
Feed from God's word, it will open up your eyes
And with confidence and conviction, His truth in you will rise

Don't let this world tell you, that there are no brighter days
Because Christ said in His word, that He is the truth and He is
acquainted with all of our ways

Moved by His presence, and lifted up on high
I can truly tell you, that the devil is a lie

Crossing the Line

I have tried to be a friend
And I have tried to understand
What you are going through

Life is too short
For any heart, to be feeling blue

Every time I think
I've got peace of mind

You turn right around
And cross the line

I do not know
What to do

How do I help?
Without hurting you

How do I help? Without feeling blue

Is there hope? Because I don't know what to believe
Because so many times, this friend is deceived

With nowhere to turn and nowhere to hide
Jesus, Jesus, be our guide

Stop these lives, from crossing the line
Please help us, one more time

D.C.

Traffic, rush hour, metro and planes, tall buildings, city blocks, people and trains, sidewalks, traffic lights vendors, and you, simple routines that the day takes you through, elevators, secured doors, carpet, and alarms, flashing lights, on every floor, that light up and warn, air conditioning, heat, and lots and lots more, computers, desks, hallways, lanes, sirens, fire trucks, ambulances and other things, Historic sights, Congress, President Obama, in the White House, telephone ringing, daughter on the other end, fingers on the mouse, Philly cheesesteak, ruffles with ridges, coke and a smile and a grin, oh and Leah, never far from my mind.

Daddy's Girl

To you, I might still be a stranger, but I am also your friend
I've been your daddy forever, at least since your life began

I will always love you Leah, in spite of the trials we face
And we will always be together, through God's mercy and His grace

Leah you are my baby, you've grown into a beautiful girl
You are smart, and bright, and beautiful, a woman to be reckoned with
in this world

Thank God that you know who your Daddy is, and thank God that you
still have peace of mind
Thank God that He watches over you, thank God your heart is so kind

You are special, and don't you ever take a back seat to life
You say that you believe in yourself, then also believe in the Christ

The truth can be very painful, and the truth can set you free
The truth can wake you up in the morning, and the truth can supply all
of your needs

My little Leah, as smart as she can be
All because she knows who she is, God has opened her eyes to see

Dead Bones Crying

I wait for an opportunity
That might come my way

But Dead Bones Crying
Trying to mess up my day
Have something else to say

I clean out my closet
With my heavy heart

My blood pressure's rising
Right off the chart

Dead Bones Crying
Won't leave me alone

Trapped in my mansion
But I want them gone

Dead Bones Crying
To see their graves

Trapped in the mirror
And full of rage

Then a voice tells me
To try to hang on

Because Dead Bones Crying
Don't have a home

Dead End

I have noticed a lot of traffic going by
Up ahead is a dead end, so I often wonder why

Could they be misinformed, coming into this neighborhood
And can't see their own end, even if they could

Are they looking for something special
To heal their aches and pain

Are they looking for pleasure
In that case, there is no gain

It makes me wonder about my own life
And wonder if this place, was worth the sacrifice

I think about my Mom and Dad that live upon the hill
They have gotten a little bit older, but I love them still

I am trapped in the moment, losing track of time
Being in this neighborhood, sometimes blows my mind

As traffic continues to go by, does anyone really give a damn
In this neighborhood, I just am, who I am

There will always be a dead end for people who don't care about sin
I'll watch traffic as it goes by, but I'll no longer, wonder why

Deeds and a Smile

Deeds and a smile, sugar and spice, is not going to get us, back to
paradise
Giving all that we should give, is not enough, being
Down and without can sometimes be tough
But when we look from within, to the presence of
Christ, He's going to share with us, a brand new life
We must pray, and pray, and pray, it is going to be
Alright

When we quit selling, ourselves short, and warm up,
Our cold, cold, cold heart
God's going to fix it for us, if we give Him some time,
Our wishes will be granted
He'll even give us peace of mind

When our life as we see it, is not going well, and
Everything else is falling and has fell
When we have done all, that we can do, and somehow
We still can't seem, to make it through
If we trust in God, our faith will renew

Deeds and a smile, sugar and spice, Christ in the spirit
And everything nice

Did Anyone Ever Ask Me

I was born, a little black child
Growing up in life, I had my moments to smile

But for some reason or another, some didn't like what they saw
I guess to some, it wasn't me, but being black was the flaw

I believed in my mother and father
And God said, I had it right

Run with your heart, Mack
And they will see the light

So I ran, and I ran as fast as I could
And I kept God's promise and it was good

He looked down, and smiled
He told me, Son, to sound it loud

Many years passed, and oftentimes, my heart got broken
I slowed down, but I didn't lose my token

Now I am older, I am not a child
But a strong black man, softly spoken

Throughout the years, tears often flowed
But I am a witness, because He has blessed my soul

No one ever considered, my big heart
They frowned on me when, I just wanted to do my part

Divine Intervention

I am here, and so are you, there is no time, like the present, there is no you, like me, but still, we are the same

This divine revelation, has brought us close, this reality, assures the right steps of man, but man in his haste, man in his own decision making process, has boasted without a plan

So will his cluelessness, be his fate, will his intelligence be enough, to save his soul

Will his spirit, elude him from all truth

You may not be sure, of who you are, but I am, and I will rise

Because, I am in the same likeness, as He, who has created me, and what my heart longs to be, will be enough for His love, to crash down on me

These things that are revealed, are the truth, and without acceptance of these things, nothing can move forward

My divine intervention

Don't Take Me for Granted

You live and you breathe, within me, I allow you to be
When you abuse me, you use me
I am no nickel or dime, so don't try to confuse me

Sometimes I fall, on hard times
But that is still, my peace of mind
Whatever will be, will be

I know that I am beautiful
I know that my mind, is as bright
As the stars
And when the sun shines, it heals all of my scars

There are no cloudy days, to confuse my mind
Just, the thought, of Heaven
To leave, the rest, behind

You tried to shake me, but you didn't break me
I am that mold, that defines my soul
I am the light, that makes everything right

When you look into the mirror, I am still there
There is nothing, that I fear

So don't ever take me for granted
And I will, let you live
I am in the world, but I am not yours, but His

Don't Write A Check That Your Balance Can't Handle

How many times have situations reminded us, that we shouldn't write a
check that our balance couldn't handle
But we write it anyway, then we look for God to have it dismantled

I've written a lot of checks and I'm sure, so have you
For some of us those checks, did not make it through

How many of us as Christians, have promised God that we would
change
And after our blessings came down, we couldn't even mention His name

How many times have we promised a loved one, or maybe even a friend
You watch my back, I'll watch yours, I'll be there for you to the end

Don't write a check that your balance can't handle

Preserve that life, and be humble, God's truth is on your side
We have made mistakes, but He knows that the pureness of our soul will
survive

It is never too late for us, because we are always in the game
We were born on God's team, and His record is unblemished, by His
name

We go out shopping, and run into the bargain of our lives
We want to reach down in that pocket, but will God's truth abide as we
decide

Don't write a check that your balance can't handle
Breathe, step back, it is God who holds the candle
Only He knows for sure, if that thought should be dismantled

Dry Your Tears Little One

As time continues to crochet its way throughout the universe
Our hearts also continue to weep in anticipation
That one day, our worth will awaken to its destiny

Dry your tears little one, the Lord of the universe hears your cry
Peace, be still, drop on your knees to the most High

How many years have we searched for this
How many years have our hearts been misguided from the truth

His eternal understanding waits on us, will wait on us
We are asleep under the wrong assumption, looking for a love that has
driven us to madness
And all around us, is nothing but sadness

Dry your tears little one
Life crumbles at your feet, as your opportunities lay grounded before you
The truth that you seek is at hand, closer than the very breath, that you
breathe

There is no shame in believing, there is no shame in expressing
There is no shame in loving Christ

The mediator and the finisher of our faith
He is the Great I am, way before, there was

Believe it, He does exist, therefore you are, and I am
Dry your tears little one, rise up, your time is now

Everything Is Good

Do I live this life, in my mansion in fear
Fretting over loved ones, because I care

Maybe I did, but now I won't
And I can truly say, that I really don't

Peace is priceless, I'm sure you know that
The truth will set you free, no matter where you're at

So everything is good, and everything is fine
I've settled in, I've settled down,
And I am not about to lose my mind

I'll wake up every morning, expecting to see that sun shining in
Then I'll lay down at night knowing, that Jesus is my friend

I'll say my prayers, then I'll go right to sleep
Everything is good, and I'm light on my feet

Is this a good day, oh yes it is
Because He is mine, and I know that I am His

Fitting In

So did you give in, did you get bullied, were you with the cool guys, or the nerds, were you ever heard
Were you too tall, maybe you were too short, maybe you were just too bold, maybe you didn't have a heart, but you had soul

It's not easy fitting in, but everybody would like to have a friend

I lived my life in a world where I tried to fit in
But knowing that I was different, I didn't have too many friends

I knew a long time ago, that I would grow
But not fitting in didn't change my soul

Following The Word

I am Your humble servant, as I try to follow Your word
Salvation is being preached, but it is Your voice, that I have heard

I have placed Your command, deep in my soul
I've come out from among the flock, as the billows begin to roll

I feel You in my spirit, oh, I feel You in my heart
Your words are peace and comfort
Your light shines out of my darkness

With Your loving arms around me, and my life placed in Your hands
It has given me hope and confidence, that through it all I still can stand

Following Your word, as I live it day by day
Gives me a purpose, that can't be taken away

Preachers and Teachers, Evangelists and friends
Thank you for this vision, that has come out from me, from within

For A Beautiful Woman

For a beautiful woman, this is what she do, fast and pray, and thank
God for you
As she looks up, into heaven, where her blessings are found, Her faith
keeps her lifted, her faith keeps her sound

Beautiful is the woman, and those that are therein
As her comforter confirms it, that Jesus will always be her friend

Beautiful is the day, that the Lord has made
And the price that His Son Jesus, paid for this foundation to be laid

There will be no other day, like the one she has today
But for this beautiful woman, know that her peace will be okay

Freedom And Fear

What is this message telling us, why should we fear, where is freedom, if freedom is not here
Al-Qaeda made a move, it threatened us all, we understand freedom but fear has no law

America now is a shaken nation, she is shook to her core, because of nine-eleven, she needs the Lord even more

Ten years of memories, a time we will never forget
America believes, that al-Qaeda is still a threat

Freedom and fear, are at war, they have obsessed a nation whose language has changed who we are
It is one thing to be at war knowing who you have to kill, it's another thing to take a life, to slaughter the innocent free at will

Most of us will never forget, the significance of that day,
Though terrorism may predate our Nation's history, during this modern era, the fear won't go away

Millions of dollars have been spent, to get us back on track, but over three-thousand lives were lost, and that money won't bring them back

Fear is taught, fear is evil, fear is void, in the beginning freedom was, now fear must be destroyed

Friend of Many Colors

You are a friend of many colors
A brother with a plan

Always ready and willing
To lend a helping hand

You are a soul man and a really cool guy
Who never lets the opportunity, of sharing his love pass him by

A man of many colors that sacrifices
His time to satisfy, the need in someone's life

I've known him for such, a long, long time
And yes he is a good man, as well as a good friend of mine

He has helped me too often to overcome
When the drought of despair had covered me from the sun,

Life had poured down puddles as many problems fell
Physically and emotionally it was like a nightmare from hell

This poem is special, I need him to know
I am sometimes preoccupied, it doesn't mean that I don't appreciate him,
or pray for his soul

Thank you for the years of being my friend
But most of all thank you for the time when it all began

You are a man of many colors, you are true to your heart
Stay on your knees brother, times in our lives are short.

Glorified Saints

You glorify the Master, You glorify the Son
You've touched wounded hearts, and turned away none

You sing to them of God's praises, as you bless them along the way
And all of your efforts, will not go astray

I'm living this moment, because I know, God is real
Satisfied and blessed, because, of how He makes me feel

I am going to praise Him, as long as I may live
I am not the world's, but I am, surely His

Thank you, Savior, thank You Lord
Feeling Your spirit, is such a great reward

Singing the songs, touched by the King
Reminds me of the promises, that each one of us should bring

You glorify the Father, you glorify the Son
You glorify the Spirit, when souls are won

All of your efforts, will not go astray
Because you're living the moment, when you sing it, God's way

God Gives The Increase

We became His heirs, a long time ago
When He gave us breath, then He blessed our soul

Even though our lives, seem to take so many different turns
It is God who gives the increase, because we are His concerns

He made us special, so that the whole world could see
That we are His shining light, that's right, you and me

And when we come together, as family and friends
His love and His blessings for us, will have no end

I have experienced my fair share of death, and seen the amazing creation
of life
To me all of it is Heaven eternal, when I can follow the will of Christ

God gives the increase, and we will survive
Though the world looks down on us, our hearts become alive

Going Straight to the Source

It is about time, that we go straight, to the source
Even if we feel that, we haven't quite, finished the course

It is time for us to realize, that we control our fate
It is time for us to lead, because destiny won't wait

It is time for action, action makes us feel
Going straight to the source, makes His love so real

My Lord assures me, that peace, will be still
That He is in control, because His truth is in my will

As I journey, throughout, the realities of this land
I am glad, and I am humbled that, God chose this man,

No more wavering, no more doubt,
The truth of the matter is, I can't do without

My steps are ordered, I've gone straight to the source
My faith is anchored, because I've stayed the course

Jesus is the reason, that I get up each and everyday
He is my rock, my source, and my way

Going Through Stuff

God is completely in control, we thank Him for our trials and the
billows that roll
The devil came to kill, steal and destroy, he tries to put in check, the
Christian joy

Circumstances do come, but the word of the Lord, is never done
If we resist the devil, the devil will flee, away from your presence and
away from me

The instant, the moment, that I go through stuff
That's when my heart, is going to be lifted up

In my life, I have been probed, stripped, and robbed
But everything that I have gone through
With ever step there was God

As I look back over my life, and I gave the world my best
My body was beat and torn, and my God said, give it a rest
He had given me many gifts, that blessed my soul
And my life remains in Him, no matter where I go

To spread this love, that touches all around
The past must be dropped and truth must be found

Never let a day go by, without opening up your heart
The world is going to give you stuff, but you keep on reaching for the
sky

He Gave Me One More Day

He woke me up this morning, put me in my right mind
He gave me one more day, to settle while I still had time

The day won't be easy, neither will the path I go
But Jesus will always tell me, how the Lord is blessing my soul

He will clean my heart and spirit, as He sends me on my way
To share His tides and offerings, He gave me one more day

My steps have been ordered, my heart is full of joy
Satan will try to attack me, but I know his power has been destroyed

I'll try to reach those saints, that are lost and in despair, I'll try to let
them know, that the Lord our Savior cares

I'll thank Him for His mercy, that has filled my life with grace
I'll stay down on my knees, through the trials that I must face

He'll wipe away my tears, and then He'll calm my doubt
Glory Hallelujah, He gave us one more day to shout

Here and Now

Here and now, I will rest my soul
I will turn it over, to the only God I know

Here and now, I will wipe my eyes
With, truth in my heart, and the Lord as my guide

Here and now, I will know what to do
Because Jesus is my anchor, when I am feeling blue

Here and now, my thinking, says I'm down
But trusting in the Lord, I know I am, Heaven bound

Here and now, is all that there is
We are dying daily, but He wants us to be His

Here and now, is sooner or later
Everything that we need, He is our, determinator

Here and now, I say, speak the truth
I'm not just talking to the Old, but I am also talking to
The Youth

Here and now, is all that we got
We can live it in Heaven, or we can, live it Hot

So don't blow your blessings, don't let desire
Blow your mind
Here and now, peace in God is yours and mine

Heroes of God's Faith

I see you every day, my brother, my sister, my friend
Heroes of God's faith, that are never satisfied with life's loose ends

You don't accept compromise, you don't live life as a lie
You live to God's perfection, and never stop to ask Him why

You believe in something more precious, that the world can't see with
their eyes every day

Patience has its perfect work, and its truth won't get out of the way

Everyone in my heart is a hero, in God's Kingdom, there are no zeros

So be strong my brother, my sister, my friend
You don't always have to witness God's promises, for His love to take
you in

Sing songs of Zion, praise, His Holy name
God's Heroes have a face, this we all can claim

I love this passion in your spirit, I love the way you make me feel
Life may have some ugliness, in it, but you give it meaning that makes it
real

The Bible tells me that we are perfect, so we must strive to be complete
Break loose those shackles off your hands, and then shake that bitter
dust from your feet

Highway Fifty-Two

It stretches across the country, Highway Fifty-Two, and this is only a
small reminder
If you're just passing through
Maybe after traveling a time or two, you will find your place
But more than anything else, you need to search God for His grace

Once you get through the mountains, and through its twists and turns
If you don't learn the highway, sooner or later you'll get burned

Sometimes it's one way in, and sometimes it's one way out
You'd better know your driving skills
Because Highway Fifty-Two leaves none in doubt

Some of my best driving, has been on Highway Fifty-Two, I can take it
fast, or slow, but you can bet I've got my eyes on you

There have been a lot of accidents, and many close calls, there's only one
of two places you can end up, but my stories don't tell it all

We are all so much alike, in that we think that we can drive
What we fail to understand, is that sometimes roads have their secrets
that they hide

I am an experienced driver, who strives for the race
But Highway Fifty-Two, is certainly not the place

You might have had some problems, at the beginning or at the end
Still Route Fifty-Two, will embrace you as a friend

Its pot holes and curves, its mountains and hills
Shall always give you its best, no matter how you feel

His Life – His Purpose

Down in Little Egypt, we had to bury this pain
Of one of our own dying, but why did it have to be in vain

This tragedy has left, all of our hearts, bitter and cold
So we try to depend on God, to bring peace to our soul

We're living in this world, on borrowed time
If it can't steal your soul, it will surely take your mind

We are a family of believers, and we know it will be okay
But those who are responsible, will have a debt to pay

We all better believe, that the God in this world is real
As we mourn over one of His soldiers, who died on the battlefield

My cousin's life had a purpose, some of you might not have known that
He was made in God's image, and God still had his back

You might think that the last days that he led, was this little man that
was so afraid
But my cousin held his own, and I knew in my heart, to God he
belonged

I would speak to him as he went by, and I would see God's love in his
eyes
I felt God's presence leading him each day, and I knew then he would be
okay

This burden he carried, he carried to his grave
But I can tell you, Church, in God's time, he will raise

We will all have to bear, this cross one day
And I believe in my heart, that God will make a way

Hold Your Peace

With those tears, that are in your eyes, with your, silent cries
A past that haunts you every day that goes by
Hold your peace

You made a vow, to endure for awhile, through the muck and the clay
And all that they say, as you live and pray
Hold your peace

Christ died for you and He died for me, as I say that I love
Christ, trying to be the best that I can be
I must hold my peace

Will you give Him your time, will you give Him your heart, will
You give Him your love
Will you give Him a start
Hold your peace

Christ made it clear, that we have nothing to fear, the enemy is
Bound, so dry up your tears
Just hold your peace

If you look around, you'll know that His love is sound, joy and
Happiness, will never let you down
Hold your peace

I am happy with joy, to know that my, fear is destroyed, to
Know that God is my protector
I hold my peace

Holy, Holy, Holy

Holy, holy, holy, this is what I see
Looking in the eyes of one
Who can surely, set you free

There is so much compassion, in every word
The point you made, was certainly heard

Linking truth to the heart
And a word to the wise
Leaves no room for pity, or self-compromise

Fighting a battle, day after day
Trying to save souls, the old-fashioned way

Whether on a mountain
Or in the valley low
We still have a conscious choice, as to which way we will go

Burn in Hell, or make Heaven our home
We don't have to be foolish, or be alone

We can spread our wings and fly away
Holy, holy, holy, God is calling on us today

Hooked On Drugs

I see it every day, Lord, in this world of mine, so many innocent lives
lost, dead and left behind

So many hurting families, even some people that I know, have stepped
into a world of darkness
That is trying to corrupt their soul

What can I do Lord? As their pain burns deep in me
And the evil, as I see it, will not let them be

Lord you have the answers, it is your peace, that I am trying to find
They are getting weaker, what prayer, will ease their mind

My heart has been heavy, my days long and sure
I know that you, can heal them
Like you healed me, many times before

It is true, that they are hooked Lord, it is true, that they have gone astray
I want to be their light, Lord, and let them know that it will be okay

Dry up their tears Lord, then please dry up mine, please show them the
way Lord, their choices are not leaving them much time

How Can You Tell a Viper

Stunning, and cunning, your everyday Joe, easy on the
Eyes, witty enough to control
A true heart breaker, evil, yet kind
They are always ready, to take what they find

Their souls never rest, and their thoughts never slow down
You can tell a viper, because their foundation is never sound
Are you this luring viper, do you concede, are you
Damned to the earth, with nowhere to feed

Do you recall the story of Moses, him and the burning bush
Still he longed for God, and God told him, "Moses, you need a push."
Everywhere that he stepped, God told him it was Holy ground
And the Lord said to him, "Take these commandments back down."

Things are not always, what they seem to be
But if they are not about God, then they are not about
You or me

A viper is always climbing, for the power of higher ground
and when they realize that there is none
then they just curse the host that they have found

How Sixteen Can You Be

How sixteen is the boy, who will become a Man
Or the girl who already has a plan
Who has pledged their loyalty, by doing
The very best that they can
How sixteen are they, will they have
The sixth sense to feel
All of the wonderful things, that are in this world
And only react, to what is real
How sixteen can you be
When love sets you free
And you are able to climb heights
That not too many others will ever see
You have a Father, who is proud
Of His child
A Father who will not stop
Until the love He gives, pours over the top
You have a family who is reinforced
By the grace of God
A family that will not stand by
And let your joy be robbed
You are, a good friend, my friend
And blessings come to those who know
That God will be with them
In mind, body and soul

I Believe

I believe of the scripture and of the human race, and the Bible which
was written
By inspired men of heavenly grace
Divinely given, and blessed at God's command, revealing the principles,
by which we all shall stand
God is the Author, salvation is its end, without mixture of error, it is the
key from a life of sin
I believe in this living God, where man's blessings and his fruitfulness,
cannot be robbed
Intelligent and spiritual, the Preserver and Creator of life
And the all knowing one, whose Son so paid the price
Infinite and holiness, we owe the highest love, who saved the world of
mankind, through the spilling of His blood
Man was created in God's image, but his sin saw him fall
Genesis plainly said, that man had dominion over it all
Man was formed from the dust of the ground, who became a living,
breathing soul
When God's breath breathed in him, his spiritual truth was told
But because of his transgressions, he fell right out of grace
Time brought him closer, to the death that he had to face
Salvation came along, gave him an escape, from his sin
Where man's posterity that he had inherited, gave God hope again
Jesus, born of the Virgin Mary, who is holy and divine, died on that
cross that day
For your sins and mine
He rose up from the grave, in His perfection of His soul
Where eternal life should have been established, as yours as well as my
goal
When we turn away from sin, we are acquitted and we are blessed
The justification of our faith, should have put all of our doubt to rest
Endowed with power, we do have peace and control
And the spirit of Christ, to calm our very soul
The assurance of salvation, through the Gospel is free
But it is our oath and duty, to be the best that we can be

I Am Young

I am young, but I am wise
If you knew my heart
It would open up your eyes
I love my father, he loves me
But still there is a whole world that I want to see
I am vulnerable, I am strong
But you are the reason, that I carry on
I love my mom
She is my life
I am so grateful for her advice
She introduced me to Christ
She is my hero, and she is my friend
She taught me to appreciate
Who I am from within
I am optimistic, I will succeed
And all that is not right
God won't let it be
Mom, Dad, and those that I love
Are my blessings, which were sent from above
I wish that you and I, could feel the same
Because a disciple of God, is not ashamed
I want to travel this world, and teach what I know
And share the same love, that I feel in my soul
Loving my community, being honest, and having trust
Having so much joy, it makes me want to bust
I am good, and I will continue to laugh, because my life
Is unwritten, and this is the appreciation that I have

I Can't Make It Without Love

I know God created me, gave me the whole world to oversee,
Put love in my heart
And said to be the best, that I can be

I'm striving to be strong, but I know, I can't do it alone
I can't make it, without love

I am tried on every side, I have God as my guide, I'm still pressing on
But I can't fight this battle with you gone
I can't make it, without love

I woke up this morning, had you on my mind, went about God's
business, wandering, hopelessly throughout time

Trying to calm the hold, that had been pressed down on my soul
But I can't, make it, without love

Jesus is my friend, the devil is a lie, I am blessed, and my Savior, the
most High

My Comforter hears me, wipes the tears from my eyes, puts me on a
path, that will help my spirit rise

He tells me that He loves me, because love can't be denied
Truth is all I have, and truth is no surprise

Now pray to the Father, and pray to the Son
You can make it, because love and truth are one

I See Prosperity Everywhere

In the grass and in the trees, I see it in you and I see it in me, I see prosperity, that you would never believe, but don't take it for granted, or you will be deceived

I see God's blessings, and I know that He cares, wherever there is love, God is there

I have seen it under the earth, I see it high in the sky, I see it when there is death, even when we don't know why

Everything, that you go through, even the things, that you're going to do, I see prosperity

Somebody get, a hold of me, because the truth as I see it, is going to set somebody free

I see prosperity

I Sing To Remember and Not To Forget

I stand here in the presence, of my God and man
The shackles have been broken, from my feet and hands

I sing to remember and to never forget
The shackles are broken, but I must still face the enemy's threats

Life is hard, there's no other way around the pain
But our blood line has existed, and it was not in vain

We are wonderfully different, and our will is strong
Respect to our forefathers, does encourage us to carry on

President Obama
He sung his songs, and never forgot
Because his belief in God, wouldn't let him stop
And he grabbed that dream, all the way to the top

We are losing control, and this won't be all, we must stand for a purpose,
that will never let us fall
Sing and be strong, to the truth that is known
Because the will that we carry, will never leave us unprotected or alone

The time is now, are there faithfuls to be found
The world is full of trouble, but don't let that get you down

Sing those songs to remember and never forget
All that we have gone through, God is not finished with us yet

I Was Chosen

In the scheme of God's plan, I was chosen

I was chosen to lead, chosen to heal
Chosen to know the difference
Chosen to do God's will

I looked and I dressed, but not to impress
While my heart abides, in this resting place
Filled with God's mercy, so I can see Him face to face

God charged His angels, to watch over me
And they shared their knowledge and I went out to set it free

I traveled the roads knowing, but not 100% sure
Until God settled me down, for the trials that I had to endure

Everything after that, became plain, simple, and clear
Traveling through the shadows, there was nothing for me to fear

I was chosen, and I became that light, for the whole world to see
My heart rushed, as the truth, stilled me

Being put on a path, to do God's will
Is a breath of Heaven, that I know, I must fulfill

I Wiped The Tears From My Eyes

Last night I wept, then I wiped the tears from my eyes, I realized that
how I was feeling, no one but Jesus, would hear my cries

I knew that Jesus, would be looking down, so I fell to my knees
Until His arms covered me all around

I looked back and thought about my cousin, who had passed away, I
thought about my Uncle, on that dreadful day

I thought about my Daddy, who was getting old, I thought about my
mama, Lord, please bless her soul

I thought about the lost, it broke my heart, I thought about my little
girl, how bright and how smart
I thought about Sarah, in an unknown land, oh dear Lord, please guide
their hands

I thought about you, then I thought about me
I thought about the world, who didn't care to see

I knew that Jesus, would be looking down, so I fell to my knees
Until His arms covered me all around

I got up, and wiped the tears from my eyes, I realized that no one but Jesus
Would hear my cries

So as I humble myself, through this valley as I go
I pray that the Lord, will continue blessing their soul

I pray that the Lord, will make a way right now
I pray that whoever is searching, will be found

I pray that God's truth, will lead them on
I pray that He fills their heart, with a place that they can call home

I Worried For So Long

After a while, it began to take its toll
I lost sight, of one important goal

I worried for so long
I didn't know, where I belonged
It was the strength of Your love, that kept me going on

I began, to resent myself
And the things, that I had to do

I fell down, on my knees
Because I had lost sight, of You

I am asking for forgiveness
As I put my doubt to rest

Lord, You are my Savior
On my knees, I do confess

I had lost sight, of one important goal
It changed my life, and turned my feelings cold

But I know, that You will help me, make it right
I worried for so long, and now I see the light

Lord, You are my Savior, please hold my hand tight
I am lost without Your love, thank You for giving me back, my sight

I'm Here To Tell You That I Love You

I'm here to tell you, that I love you
I'm here to tell you, that I need you so
I'm here to tell you, you're always on my mind
I'm here to tell you, I will never let go

I see the love, that's in your eyes
I have the touch, that satisfies
Like when it rains, or the warmth from the sun
Julia Anne, you're the only one

I'm here to tell you, that I love you
I'm here to tell you, that I need you so
I'm here to tell you, that you are always on my mind
My heart skips beats, and I lose track of time

Make a wish, and follow the stars
I'll be there, wherever you are
I find myself, drifting with the clouds
Where true love will never let us doubt

I'm here to tell you, that I love you
I'm here to tell you, that I need you so
The years may come, and then they're gone
But a love like ours, will live on and on

You and I, can hear our song, as our hearts just beat along
You and I, will praise His name, on a cloud where our love is the same
Julia Anne, I Love you

I'm More Sure Today Than
I was Yesterday

I am more sure today, than I was yesterday, so doubt, confusion and
loneliness
Get out of my way

My steps have been ordered, my vision is clear
I am more sure today, than the doubt that appears

It's talking to you, that seems to soothe my soul
Our conversations restore my life, that otherwise seems to get old

You are my miracle, and my peace, still
You are the smile and the laughter, and the food that I feel

Everything about you, makes my journey in me so real
I'll tell doubt, and confusion, it's time for me to heal

I am more sure today, than I ever will be, because I talk to my spirit
And I am, set free

Try harder, reach higher, listen to the spirit's command
Being sure of yourself today means, that your life, is in God's hands

It Has Always Been A Dream Of Mine

It has always been a dream of mine, to talk to people, who have
encouraging minds
It has always been a dream of mine, to settle up, and leave, the past
behind
It has always been a dream of mine, to lift up, precious souls
To speak from a place that's sacred, where speaking to the truth, never
gets old
It has always been a dream of mine, to share love that others could not
see
To dream a dream worth living, that has burned passionately in you and
me
It has always been a dream of mine, to see the same sparkle in
everybody's eye
That sparkle that lights up across the sky, that sparkle that opens
Heaven, near and wide
It has always been a dream of mine, that we would remember this day
over and over again
A day where truth is set in motion, and we define ourselves as friends
It has always been a dream of mine, to see my parents up on that hill
And to open up my eyes, to see, that this dream, was for real

Jealousy and Gossip

Jealousy and gossip, we know that it can kill
But jealousy and gossip, won't win you Calvary's hill

It is hurtful, so gossip, be still
Jealousy has no place, but its sting can be for real

Backbiting and slanderous, is this how you deal
You can't destroy God's perfect harmony, so peace, be ye still

You will never keep a friend, that will understand
Unless you are dancing with the devil, and shaking Satan's hand

Get up and get moving, get out, of the way
Or the Lord, will blast you, and everything you say

Maybe you missed the joy, because you had, a bad life

Maybe you turned to a friend, who gave you bad advice

Whatever the reason, Jesus is here now, if you are looking for a Savior,
He won't let you down

For jealousy and gossip, it will never have a place
But for the word of Jesus, it'll meet you face to face

Just Throw Me a Line

Please show me the way, by the end of the day
And I know in my heart, that it will be okay
Help me to be strong, when my thoughts go wrong

Just throw me a line
I'll catch it this time

I got things on my mind
I don't want to be left behind

I made a promise, a long time ago,
When God blessed me, that I still would grow

When I fell short, God saw my heart
Just throw me a line
And I'll come up out of the dark

I'll give to the poor, that I see each day
Knowing that You, Lord, will make a way

Help me to be strong, when my thoughts linger on
Just throw me a line
I know all hope ain't gone

Kin and Friends

What's so special, about kin and friends
With them their love, will never end

Some of them live, so far away
But still come together, to make each other's day

Some have come, to show what a family really means
Because in God's eyes, a family is everything

A lot of people, have come together as kin
And right along side them, are their friends

They made the trip, with this special day in mind
To share this moment, and leave their troubles behind

Young and the old, so thankful for the years
Never take for granted, the love that is here

When we treat them with respect, we'll see the joy in their eyes
And know that God's love, is no surprise

Knocked Down But Not Knocked Out

This realistic world that we live in, is spiritually blinded because of the
lack of its faith
It has become routinely programmed, not wanting to know what truly
awaits

Will the teacher become the student, will the lesson ever be learned
Knocked down but not knocked out, seems to be our only concern

Living in a society where the truth is assumed, and very seldom told
Has put us in a state of mind, that could do so much damage to our soul

Believing is the beginning, retribution may be the end
But being about our Father's business, could one day be our only friend

Being wise has its advantages, like a clock that ticks throughout time
But if you don't put that battery in, that clock like life, just becomes
another state of mind

I'm not looking for any confessions, and I don't have any regrets
Knocked down but not knocked out, is something that my soul never
frets

I rise above my fears, with a little help from the Lord, ever since I have
been converted
I look to Heaven, for my reward

Leaving The Milk Weed

There were times on the mountain
When following the Word
Had me afraid to go back down
Because I didn't think that I'd be heard

Too much violence and corruption, was down below
There was hell to pay, wherever I go
Too much darkness Lord, but I am still your seed
Can I be transformed from the milky weed

It's been ugly, will you strip away the mess
It's time to spread my wings and leave the nest
You allowed me to climb, to the mountain top
Now You tell me the pity, and doubt must stop

You say it's okay, to meditate in this place
That the valley is where, I find my mercy and grace
As I looked into Heaven for signs, You touched my hand
To tell me that hope, is in the Promised Land

You say to leave the mountain, cross the valley, touch every soul
Try to mend every heart, including the broken and the cold
And to stand on the Promises, I made to You that day
And nothing, or no one, will ever get in Your way

I know that there's darkness but I am still Your seed
Let me be transformed, from this world, out of the milky weed

Lest We Forget

All that we have is today, lest we forget, that the God of our
Creation, is not done with us yet

We give praise to a people, whose legacy will stand, whose
Blood, sweat, and tears, helped to build this great land

In giving honor and praise, our children will learn
That hope without purpose, can ruin the intent of God's plan
Through many blessings, that the enemy didn't rob
Our future became as real, as the people that it involved

People who bled and died, who never saw color
People who took on so much, and defended one another

Amazing people, who were never ashamed, as they shouted and praised,
the Savior's name
Good people, who always had a song, as they sung about their
Visions, that kept them pressing on

These great men and women, meeting down by the riverside,
With so much more to live for, with nothing left to hide

Enslaved and in bondage, for all those many years, if you
Really had a conscience, it would bring your eyes to tears
Lest we forget, the God of creation, is not through with us yet

Know, that we can do more than pray, we can raise awareness,
By being a better person each day
This is a time, when we should be bowed down at God's throne
Learning, as we move forward, remembering about a people,
That stood proud and strong

Listen To The Spirit

I woke up this morning after I had rested in His word
With the voice of God telling me, it is time that He be heard

I had a flashback like Moses, at first I was afraid, until the Lord opened
up my mouth and said
The foundation has been laid

People get ready, God's time is at hand, it has been spoken for
generations
Here cometh the Son of man

I prayed about that spirit that rested inside of me, I rested on His word
It's time to set it free

Jesus is calling for all to come Home, lay your heavy burdens down
And rest them at His throne

It is not too late, but time is still at hand
Please swallow your pride, and confess Him while you can

I was set free, from a turmoil of pain, everywhere I turned everything
just seemed the same

My burdens were heavy and my heart was not light
Until you filled me with your love Lord, so my spirit could keep heading
right
Rested in His word folks, I truly heard His call
Telling me to get ready, because Satan's walls were going to fall
Praying to God, has put my mind to rest
With the voice of Jesus telling me, it is time to be at my best

Live By Example, How You Believe

The mistake that most of us make, is always trying to listen to other
opinions, opinions that have no weight, so then life calls us out
Our voices, must be the voices of our hearts, and not of doubt

We should live by example, of how we believe, although at times, we still
may be deceived

We must be the example of the things that mean the most, then in joy
and truth, our hearts will always boast

Live by example, it is what you believe
Cross over into Jordan on your knees, you will receive

Living My Mama's Pain

There is no pleasure in this
As I live my Mama's pain

I sometimes shed a tear
Because of the things that can't be explained

Hope is all she has to lean on everyday
Sometimes the stress of my burdens seem to get in her way

I watch her and it seems like, she's living in a glass
With no way to turn, and her air is leaving fast

Where is her comfort, it is very seldom shown
Living my mama's dream in pain that is not the way anyone should go

All she wants is a little love as each day goes by
Why can't she find comfort, at least my mama tries

I live for the day, that she is no longer in pain
Praise God, Hallelujah, bless her just the same

Look, Feel, and Believe

You can look in their faces and see the story of their lives
In it is heartache, loneliness, and strife

You can sense the struggles, that life has put them through
And then you know, why their expression seems so blue

You can believe in their voices, as you feel their pain
Then you pray to God, that their life is not in vain

They can lean, on God's everlasting arm
Or get swept up by life's troubles, pitfalls, and swarms

We can ask for a prayer, or a blessing or two
When there are times like these that, they don't know what to do

We can take matters into our own hands, or thank grace and mercy
For the hope of the Promised Land

We can set in our quiet places, or open up our hearts
We can hold on to our burdens, or believe that the healing will start

We can set and doubt about the gossip that we hear
Or pray to the Lord, that His blessings become clear

There is always a point of no return
But it doesn't have to be, if you bow down and learn

Give God the glory, the hope, and the pain
Look, feel and believe, that He will take care of everything

Looking Up

As I look up at this crowd, with your smiling face, I am very happy to be
here, in such a wonderful place
To share with you the love, and the joys of life, and the peace that we
get, when our hearts are right

I'm the G-Man, and I'm here to say, our town is healing better, because
we share more love today

We're brothers and sisters, we're family and friends, we are the hope for
tomorrow, that never ends

We are a light for the future, and a chance for tomorrow, we're reaching
for the stars, we're not down in our sorrows

Our time has come, and we won't play it down, we've waited long
enough, and we want it now

Hotels, motels, good roads and stores, Greyhound buses
And trains like we had before

Because as I look up at this crowd, with their smiling faces
I know that God has blessed us, with His mercy and His grace

I'm the G-Man and I am here to say, look up everybody, because
tomorrow is another day

Lord Be My Guide

Through the mist and the rain
When my heart cries in vain, be my guide

When my whole world crumbles and I seem to stumble
Lord, be my guide

Because the time has come, for me to stand
Lord, be my guide, and hold my hand

When I know I've crossed over
Into a foreign land

Please deliver me
Where I stand

Lord, be my guide, hold my hand
Comfort me now, from the evil eyes of man

Rest Your hand upon my shoulder
Make me wise, pure and bolder

Lord, be my guide

Lord, What Have You Given Me Today

You woke me up this morning
You put a smile on my face

I am absorbed in You
So there are no dreams that I have to chase

To live in such a freedom
And to be there when You call

Is like looking in a mirror
And knowing you have it all

I am thankful for this moment
That put my mind at ease

And I am happy for this day
Enjoying Your fall-time breeze

You protect me in my sleep
Then You allow me to wake up again

You share with me a blessing
That only You can give a man

Love the Life You Live

The road we travel
May not always be straight

So know the difference
Between love and hate

Keep an open mind
It will elevate your soul

And never lose track
When your heart is set on your goal

The mountains we climb, might not be no higher
Than the thoughts of our mind

So when we make a decision
Don't be caught off guard

Make sure that the truth we are looking for
Becomes our only reward

Still the road we travel, and the chances we take
Will make the difference, between love and hate

Love the life that you live
And let the Lord do His will

Made Up In My Tent

You sent me a blessing Lord, it came in many forms
You opened up hearts, Lord, so kind and so warm

Just like the colors of a rainbow, did each person's spirit touch my soul
I have seen the gleam in their eye, it's not about me but the cross where
You died.

Your blood that was shed upon that cross, should have opened eyes of
those who were lost

It should have changed their lives, like the parting of the sea
That saved a wretched soul like me

You might not be weeping, Lord, but I am sad
Losing any soul is bad

I am born again, not by the blood of man but by the chastisement of my
sin
I have felt the depths of Hell, but Your praying souls have done me well

Each night as I die away to sleep, it's your awesome spirit that makes me
weep
I weep sometimes, all night long, just wishing to be one of those present
on Your throne
But I know, I still have a mighty job to do
Trying to reach every heart, 'til they follow You

Mama To You, I am Thankful

Mama to you, I am thankful, for all of the things that you have done
I am proven, and I am blessed, I am your wise, and obedient son

Mama I can't even imagine, myself not walking up on that hill
To move your arms and legs, because, I know your pain is real

I wish that there was more, that I could really do, Mama I know that
you hurt, but I don't know what, you are going through

I don't know why God picked you, you have been faithful to all that you
know

But I can tell you this, you have been a blessing to my soul
I love it when you ask me to come and move your arm or your hands, I
like it even more when I become your feet to stand
I know this life must be hard, I know being humble can sometimes
cause you to break

You are truly an angel, and a mother in whom I am so proud
Success as you have shown me, has made me more humble as God's
child

Mercy Me

My eyes have seen, my ears have heard
There is trouble in the camp, mercy me, that's the word

I have felt her impact, I have tasted her spoil
But I was touched by an Angel, mercy me, Oh my Lord

I put on my look, I changed my wear, a new day has come
So I must always be aware

Mercy me, I am one with the Lord
Better days are ahead, because He comes with His reward

Truth has no burden, it is the light of the world
And it's given to all of us, mercy me, even boys and girls

There are no setbacks, I accept no shame
Mercy me that's the truth, I say it in Jesus' name

Yes my eyes have seen, and my ears have heard
There is trouble in the camp, but I don't believe a word

I am going to keep pushing; I am going to make it through
Mercy me, mercy you, we all have favor, and God loves us too

Mine to Have

I want to know who I am
Am I a child of Abraham?
I want to know the truth they sought
And at what price was it bought.

Wandering the desert, homeless and stranded
Each one of God's people had been branded.
But they endured with the faith instilled,
Knowing that it was God's will

Up on the top of Calv'ry Hill
Between two thieves, the wind stood still.
A whispered cry, an anguished plea
"Why, God, have you forsaken me?"

God's promise has always been
A covenant between all men.
For all who choose to believe
They will have life eternally.

I want the blessings from above.
I want to be wrapped up in God's love.
Am I a part? Is it mine to claim?

"Yes, my child," God did proclaim.

(Written by Julia Anne Edwards)

Mom and Dad

These words will only describe, a small portion of how I feel
I want you to know, Mom and Dad, that my heart is real

You have sacrificed so much, and instilled this love in me
I try to live this truth, that only the blessed will see

I am giving you your flowers, while I still can
And I am thanking you for this love, that has inspired me as a man

Because this love runs deep, I am grateful and blessed
I am more than a conqueror, you taught me to accept nothing less

I look into the heavens, where I see my reward
And I know that life's struggles, don't have to be hard

I thank you respectfully for my life, I thank you truly for your sacrifice
But most of all, Mom and Dad, thank you for introducing me to my
Lord and Savior, Jesus Christ

Words can be important, with the messages that they bring
And this message is to let you know, that you will always be my Queen
and King

Two beautiful people, who are living their lives
Who have touched many hearts, and who have opened up many eyes

I am the living proof, that the Son will rise
So I am giving you your flowers, because the truth has opened up my
eyes

Mowing Grass

I set out this morning to cut my grass, at the crack of dawn
My back was hurting, but I still pressed on
Pulled out the mower, and the gas was low
My blood pressure was up, but I still had to go

So I went downtown, to get some gas
Talked to a couple people, that made me laugh
We shot the bull, for a minute or two
Until I suddenly remembered, what I still had to do

I got that gas, and I jetted out of town
The clock was running, but it wasn't slowing the sun down
I ran that mower, up and down that yard
Five hours later, I was sweating hard
The sun was kicking, and I was heavy on my feet
At just past noon, it started to peak

I drunk some water, to try to cool down
Even in the shade, the heat had me bound

A few minutes later, I was back at it again
Mowing that grass, as fast as I can
After pushing that mower, and fighting that sun
My work this morning, was finally done

When you decide that you need to cut your grass
Beat that sun, or it will, kick your …………

My Coach, My Friend, My Mentor

A long time ago, I started a race
Hoping one day people, would notice my face
It wasn't long, when it took place
Because I had a wonderful coach, and God in my grace.

He taught me, much more than sport
Not one time, did he sell me short
For twenty-five years, we have been apart
But I still love this coach, bless his heart

He taught me things that made me strong
When I got off track, he'd knock me off my throne
This wonderful, beautiful, mentor of mine
Did more than just coach, he kept me in line

The things that I've accomplished, with my life
Helped me to understand, his sacrifice
With so much love and such a big heart
This man's compassion was off the chart

He stands for much more, than he'll ever know
He has changed more lives than any picture show
My friend, my coach, my mentor
Has raised the bar and opened many doors

Dedicated to Coach Marino, Welch High School, 1976

My Father, My Friend

Everyday, is a special day for a Dad
My Father, My Friend is not a fad

We know that he, is always there
But does he know that we, really care

And do we ever take a moment, to let him know
That we love him, even when, it doesn't show

While the sun gleams high, in the sky
While we can still open up, our mouths and eyes

Let him know how important, he is
Let him know that we are still a fan of his

A true father, of us all
Might watch us slip, but he will never let us fall

His mercy and His grace, are all over the place
That is why in this life, trouble shouldn't be so hard to face

Again he loves us, through the good times and the bad
So with a father like this, who should ever be sad

He is the reason, that we carry on
And his love never ceases, even when we think all hope is gone

Can there be such a day, for a Dad
I know that there is for mine, he's the best friend, that I ever had

My Two-Mile Walk

I do it early in the morning, when most folk are still in bed, my two-
mile walk, gives me a chance to clear my head
Since I live in the country, things go bump in the night, so I take my
walking cane, and follow the path where there are lights
Where I live at in the mountains, there are green trees all around
I walk on one-o-three, but wild animals still come down
I guess they are as curious, as sometimes I feel, but I can't let strange
noises, change my heart, or my will
For many health reasons, I try to keep up with the pace
Early in the morning, I seek God's mercy and His grace

Right up the road, there are fenced-in dogs gone wild
Me and my walking stick, just pass them with a smile
The morning comes early, but I am always on my way
Trying to stay healthy, so that I can see another day
A mile down the road, I circle around the bank trying to keep some
order, of the way that I should think
Back on one-o-three I'm just a few feet from home, forty-five minutes is
about how long I have been gone
I throw my dog a treat, as I come into the gate
It's five o'clock in the morning, as I take off my training cape

Night Time Falls

Night time falls, I'm alone in the dark, as I look to Jesus, who has my heart
I look up the hill, my parents' lights are on, I press up that hill, even if I have to face the unknown

It is late in the evening, about eleven o'clock, a little dew forms, then begins to drop
My heart is telling me not to wait, to follow my fate, Dad's putting Mom to bed, so there is no debate

The mountains here are high, the shadows are deep, everything on earth is probably crawling, around my feet, and nothing is asleep

I've taken this route before, many times in the past, fear had come on me, but with God, fear didn't last
Though my thoughts seem to wander, my heart pounding fast, I heard a noise up ahead, something is in their trash

At night, bears have been seen, and other wild game, but I press on, in Jesus' name

He holds my hand, He comforts my soul, He directs my path, though the billows may roll

I will reach their house, and I will help tuck Mom into bed, then I will gently lay a couple of pillows, right under her head

I'll say good night to my Dad, then cut off the lights, knowing that my God is an awesome God, and the Ruler, of both day and night

Nightmare on Elm Street

Sometimes you think that, you know someone
Who means the world to you

Then comes a Nightmare on Elm Street
But that kind of thing won't do

You pray that things would change
And that your respect would lead the way

Because having a Nightmare on Elm Street
Is not going to make things okay

Nights without sleeping, and worry on your mind
Make you wonder if Freddie, is not far behind

I won't continue being his victim
In spite of the way things have been

A Night on Elm Street with Freddie
Who in the world needs friends

I created this illusion and this abuse must go
Out from my thinking, and on with peace for my soul.

As a nightmare on Elm Street
Won't be anymore

Not My House, But His

I live in this mansion, as humble as I can be, this is not my house, but
His mansion, I oversee

I'll keep it clean, and polished, as I stay down on my knees, this is not
my mansion, but His house, I oversee

Sometimes I might get weary, but I know my heart is right
I'll praise my Lord and Savior, morning, noon, and night
Do you have your house together, is your mansion, fresh and clean
Is it swept and is it polished, because God's House, is everything

This is the beginning, or could this be the end
You can be the rightful owner, of faith among all men

This may not be your house, but keep it the best that it can be
When God gave you this life, He gave you, this mansion to oversee
Not my house but His, His will, will be done
I oversee this mansion, because He told me, that I was the one

Our Hope is More Than That

Setting here on my front porch, a revelation came, then left
I am blessed beyond measures, I'd like to add that blessing of hope, to
someone else

As I looked across the tracks, directly in front of me
There are a group of people, whose actions have shown that what they
are doing shouldn't be

What can I do Lord, my cup has overflowed, Jesus I love you, please
help their belief to grow

I'll stay down on my knees, and I'll pray just a little more
Pray that their hearts will hear you, knocking, knocking at the door
The warmth of the sun shines down on my face, this late October day
Lord, you are the truth, and I know you will make a way

My heart beats intensely, my tears just want to fall
As I desperately try to hold them back, words of encouragement start
to call

My love for Jesus, makes that hope real
Our hope is more than that, it is hope that makes us feel

Precious Savior, the true Father of us all
Who sends down His blessings, whether they are big or small

I set on my porch, knowing that Jesus is just a breath away
I thank Him for the joy, of seeing another beautiful day

I thank Him for the courage, that has made my life complete
But most of all I thank Him, trusting that my faith will always keep

Our Purpose

The Christian will tell you, that God made us all
The world will tell you, that the weak will fall

Life will tell you, that experience is the way
God's word will show you, that everything will be okay

It is most natural, to want peace of mind
Or to want to know where we came from, what we lost, that we must
find

There is a much broader picture, that we should see
Christ came and died on the cross, for you and for me
He gave us direction, then He wiped away our fears
Standing on the word of God, makes everything else so clear

We do have a purpose, and it's our gift to claim
We have Holy Ghost power, and we believe it, in Jesus' name

Being recognized by an angel, that God has sent
Is definitely a calling, for us to repent

Through His love, we should remember and know
That a heartbeat with Spirit, can bring blessings to a soul

The bad might get ugly, the bad might get cold
The bad has no purpose, and the good won't let it grow

The bad, a forgotten memory, that got lost in time
Looking for its purpose, that is not far behind
Be a blessing to others, and you will be a blessing to yourself
And you will know that in Christ, there is, nothing else

Perfect Wonder

The clouds try to hide, God's amazing skies
But like the truth, the sky won't be denied

When the fullness of time, stops cold in our life
Know that our Savior, is still, Jesus Christ

Our Perfect Wonder, Our King of Kings
He has given us the victory, even in our dreams

So believe, that your sun will rise
And believe, He'll wipe, the tears from your eyes

Believe in your heart, that there's a, brighter day
The Lord is our refuge and He will make a way

I pray that you reach, for the Master's hand
And let His spirit in you, guide the man

He is Lord, within our lives, He is our strength
No other will suffice

He is our beginning, and He is our end
He's a Perfect Wonder, and He is still our friend

Don't worry Brother; God's angels won't lead you astray
But speak with conviction and it will be okay

He is our Lord, and He is God of all
Don't forget that the Father, can break down hidden walls

He's Our Perfect Wonder; He's our King of Kings
He's the Joy in my heart, He's the music that it brings

Perilous Times

These are our Perilous times, and without the faith of our Savior, our world ends, yours and Mine

There is no other power greater, than that of Christ
As the old man dies daily, to a new way of life

Men of all color, easily do we forget
We may not believe in Him, but He is not done with us yet

God made us a promise, then handed us the key
God took in account, that we would be blinded by what we see

But God blessed us anyway, even through these Perilous times
He gave us back our peace, that He knew we'd leave behind

Jesus, you're my Father, and I am your Son
Guide me through this confusion, Perilous times or none

I look within my heart, and my soul cries out
I will have faith, and Lord, I will not doubt

Poison

They were called the invincible fat boys, some say the Iraq twins
Over eight hundred pounds of terror, who cheated their lives before it
began

They manipulated others, enticing them to sell their souls
Not for the price of eternal life, but for worldly pleasures, silver, riches
and gold

They made thousands of dollars, on their way to the top
But they had no peace, because they were always haunted by the cops

The less fortunate and the innocent, had become their slaves
Stripped of their virtue, with one foot in the grave

Blinded by their senses, addicted to that life
Poisoned by the effects of their success, they couldn't hear the voice of
Christ

If you are running away from anything, don't forget where you belong,
remember, Princess, there is no place like home
Because in this ghetto, you are here today, and then you're gone

Slavery is over, but it carries a brand new face
It is ultimately poison, that destroys the human race

If you are looking for a good time, you'd better think that through
The Iraq twins are invisible, but they still have their eyes on you

Push On

When my tears just wouldn't hold back and I hurt so bad I thought that
I would crack
I just pushed on
When it had been so hard for me to please
After all the times when I had been deceived
I just pushed on

When I was down to my last dime
So broke that I almost lost my mind
I just pushed on

When life had me by the threads
And all I wanted to do was lie down in bed, and put the covers over my
head
I just pushed on

When I was so in need of a friend
And my walls started crashing in
I just pushed on

But I remembered what my mama said
And I got myself back up, out of bed
I just pushed on

I know that Jesus is my friend, watching over me all the time
Even when I am at my end,
I push on

When life had me by the threads
And my walls came tumbling down, no friend could be found

And I remembered what my mama said
That Jesus was alive and hope wasn't dead
I push on

Rested on His Word

I woke up this morning after I had rested on His word
With the voice of Jesus telling me, it is time that He is heard

Just like Moses, at first I was afraid, until He opened my mouth and said
The foundation has been laid

People get ready, time is at hand, spoken for generations
Cometh the Son of man

I listened to the spirit that rests inside of me, I've rested on His word
Now it's time to set it free
Jesus is calling for all to come Home, lay your heavy burdens down
And leave them at His throne

It isn't too late but know that time is at hand
Rest on His word and believe that Jesus can

He'll pick you up, when you are down
And let you know that you are special now

And when you are up, He'll keep you there
If you are resting in His word, you'll never have a care

Real Love

Have you ever had the pleasure, of experiencing time standing still, have you ever experienced how another person, really makes you feel

No one can teach you, you have to trust your heart to believe
Because real love is so special, that it will bring you to your knees
I am a witness, to what this love can do
I am on top of the world, and it can happen for you

Real love will find you, when your heart is working right
Don't you settle for artificial love, because you won't see the light

Some people you'll enjoy their company, some people will blow your mind
Make sure it is what you need, and leave what you doubt behind

I have a friend, and her love is real to me
She once doubted, but her pure heart wouldn't let it be

God came down and touched her, He touched her heart and soul

She is a walking miracle, and she shows it, everywhere she goes

Running on a Platform of Hope

What will be the outcome in this land of the free, where change really matters in America for people like you and me
What type of men would stand between hope, and the freedom that it brings to those families less able to cope
These are the kinds of issues that bring America down, while other politicians prosper on the upper end of town
I know politicians like that, they just don't care, they would rather see America broke, down and on her knees, and in despair
I know some who still fringe on color, that has bound us for two-hundred years
Who prospered during slavery time, as America drowned in her tears
Indeed I was impressed last night when the president's speech tried to mend the differences of those in our infrastructure who need to step up and do what is right
Yes I was impressed and all of us should believe, that united we are strong and no longer will we be deceived
Some Americans have set back and seen this Country bound, and not free
Because of a changing government that supports the likes of you and me
A government built on restoring public trust should be what it's about
But then again, what party will wait around to figure that one out
The first State of the Union address, said a lot to me
Run on a platform of hope, I believe this administration will help, and can set the pace for the whole world to see

Setting in the Football Stands With My Daddy

Dad I think about our adventures, all the time, how we have weathered
many storms, even when our teams were behind
We were troopers throughout, the rains, the cold, and the winds
We both hung tough, even when our fingers didn't want to bend

Times spent with you, in those football stands, were blessings from God
You are truly a sports lover, and a real die-hard fan, you are my Dad and
I am your number one fan

But it doesn't matter what sport
Because they all have our heart
Though our bones hurt and our hair turns gray,
We'll stay young because the love of the sport won't go away

Settled and Complete

We have searched for so long, trying to find our way
Hoping that our search, will lead to a better day

Hoping that the sun will always shine, hoping that somehow, we will get
peace of mind

So we hope, then hope is gone, and wonder why the Lord has left us
alone

He hasn't, and we must believe that all is well, because in the end, we
will all have a story to tell
The story of the bad times that came our way, the story of the blessings
that didn't go astray
The story of miracles that saved a life, the story of our Savior, Jesus
Christ

Led by example, the eyes of the Lord are on you
Help bring back the joy, to so many that are blue

Because our settled look, can only be complete
When we humble ourselves, at the Master's feet

Shadows Don't Lie

As I walk through these valleys, their shadows don't lie
Evil is present, and death is nearby

I tell myself that fear, is not of God
And no treasure in Heaven, has ever been robbed

Closer to me than the wind, are unforeseen eyes
Whispers that linger, that would make a little baby cry

With cars running rapid, and tension running high you would think
that you were in a war zone, and you can't fathom why
When this kind of darkness, can stir one's heart
There is only one faith, that will never sell you short

That's the Holy Ghost presence, because God is good
He will surely take the curse, out of this neighborhood

Love your neighbors, friend, put the shadows in the light
Truth will prevail, God is right

Open up your heart, let peace be still
God is the truth, and the truth is real

Simple Illusion

Others don't express
They confuse life
They repress, not knowing
They suppress
And often they assess
But don't address
The things they possess
So that they can be harnessed
Into real assets
Which puts them
At their best

Simple Things

A beautiful sunrise, followed by a beautiful sunset
Normal times in our lives, that we will never forget

Saying to someone I love you, or yes I can
Are the simple things in life, that render the blessings of man

If we are not careful, and if we pretend to be too proud
We will miss out on the simple things, that brighten our heart and make
us smile

This church is just a building, a meeting place for you and me
But within these walls are the simple things, that show God the beauty
that He wants to see

When I feel that spirit, deep down in my soul, I know I have support,
and that feeling will never grow old
Then I know within my heart, that what I am feeling won't sell me short

God has the only solution, knowing that problems will come
But a simple thing like love, can rain down miracles from the Son

This old building has come along way, giving me peace when I had gone
astray
Now I look forward, to the simple things in life
Like honoring my Lord, and my Savior, who is Jesus Christ

Sisters

I have wonderful sisters, who mean a lot to me, our blood runs deep,
because God has let it be
We've done so much together, over the years we've all held on, our
parents had always taught us, that the Lord would keep us strong

This day has finally come, we all have families of our own
Through the grace of God, His word has set the tone

We laugh, we love, and we pray, because we know that the Lord will
make a way

I can't say enough, about how special my sisters are
I just know that in my heart, they are my shining stars
They are there when I need them, they always understand
God chose my sisters, then He placed them in special hands

As kids we grow up, from the adolescents that we were
Some people are taught to take, while others are taught to care

Thank you, God for all sisters, all over the world
I thank God for mine, and their love which is a pearl

Slow Down Boy

Whatcha hurry
Ya mama callin' your name
Missin' suppa or some other thing

Enjoy life, boy, while you can
Soon enough you'll be a man
Corns growing on your feet, callous' growing on your hand
Next thing you know, you'll be sayin' "I'm sinkin' but I'm the man"

Whatcha been up to
Still havin' problems in school
Still likin' that girl
With that big butt and curls

Slow down boy
Have a little respect
Girls ain't like toys

If ya get on their bad side
Then there ain't gonna be no place in this world to hide

Didn't ya mama teach you any better
Don't be no fool
Stay in school and remember the Golden Rule

Don't get frustrated, it will be okay
Just slow down, boy, 'n listen to what I say

Be strong in the Lord, and keep on keepin' on
Slow down boy
Have some joy
Don't be headstrong

So Close to Home

So what if I am pushed, what can I do?
It doesn't mean that I stop living
I have to push on through
Some things I can decide
Others, I have to ride
I have to hold onto something greater than me
And hope my eyes open for me to see
I have to sometimes shed tears
That will cleanse my soul
And I realize that there are reasons
Each day as time goes
Some sad moments, some bright
May keep me up all night
But it's not always easy
The life I try to lead
If I stop and think for a moment
Then I just might succeed
I have no solid answers
Why things happen the way they do
But I am totally convinced
That being so close to home
Means being so close to you

So Much to Live For

It was not the hand that I was dealt, that gave me back my life, it was
what I did afterwards, knowing that I had paid the price
At times I felt so far down, that when I looked up, I felt six-feet
underground
I was not that person that life thought they saw, I knew when God made
me, there was no flaw

So much to live for, so much to gain, I came into this world, and you
will, remember my name

And this truth will set me free, so much to live for, and so much to be

You thought that I would die, and you were right
No longer do you have a hold, for I have been redeemed into the light

I walk in confidence, to show God's glory
The truth that I live, will always tell my story

I blame no one, as I look back, God spoke love to my heart, and peace,
is where I'm at

Sold on Love

We dream of love, but will it come true
I am sold on a love, and that love is you

Not the roses or the violets, not the candy or the rings
But sweet, sweet love, and the magic that it brings

I will always be yours, and you will always be mine

Together and forever, we'll be sold on love, and time

Life will see us, boldly holding hands
We'll hug and kiss, on our way to the Promised Land

As I look into your eyes, and as I hold you tight
God will cradle us both, under His magic light
I am sold on love and that love is you
Thank you, Lord, Jesus, for this dream of love that came true

Subtle or Sovereign

In many ways, my life has changed, and still in this world, so much
remains the same
I live but I am crucified each day, my vision stays clear, so my heart
won't go astray

Though the tempter comes, subtle and quick
I stay my course, so I will never forget

My Lord knows my fears, and calms me through the storms
And my truth need not, always be alarmed

I am wonderfully, and beautifully made
I walk in the confidence, that the debt has been paid

When God woke me up this morning, He already had a plan
So my steps have been ordered, as I lean not on the promises of man
I will share with you, what I know, and I will encourage, the doubtful
soul
I will meet you, and I will greet you, because there is no defeat
In many ways, things, remain the same
But in my life, there has been a change

Life is subtle, and so is the hand of time
But for you and me, our vision remains God's truth,
sovereign and never blind

Success and Fame

I grew up in the seventies, I didn't start out to make a name, but like all of the others, I dreamed of success and fame

I was raised in the church, it was something that I loved, that kept me praising God's name

competitive running was something, that was always in my mind, I ran so well, I ran just to pass the time

Then I followed my dreams, that took me to the top, but God humbled my heart, when my times started to drop

I went to the Olympic trials, with a blown-out knee, I was still on top of the world when God said, there's more in life to be

Riches and gold, you already had, you were raised by the best, your Mom and Dad

As I humbled myself to God's voice, and to the beat of my heart, He said that it was my time, to build His ark

Again He spoke from my spirit that opened up my eye, and my soul responded, as His riches fell from the sky

I grew up with no intentions, of making a name, yet some turned their back, when truth started to spring

God kept my mind focused all of those years, just like it is today, to let me know He still cares, knowing that it's going to be okay, I'm singing and praising God, the old fashioned way

The word of God cannot be beat, in Him you will rejoice, but in the world, you will weep

Tapped Out

In the midst of all that drama, and you've come to your wit's end, don't
give up and let the dark side, of your troubled life, win
Humble yourself during that moment, God's love will filter in, how do I
know, because this is how, the healing begins

God's truth is all that we have, and the truth will set us free
Don't you dare back up, let the Savior be
God will toss and turn, those moments, and change that darkness so
you can see

In the midst of all the drama, you'll see the devil play
He'll play his tunes of misery, and try to sift your life away

I know that you're tapped out, but it's going to be okay
The healing is coming, and the Comforter is on His way

Don't let that devil win, it's a brand new day
You might be tapped out, but Jesus has tapped you as His friend
You might be tapped out, but Jesus has tapped you as His friend

The 21st Century Psalmist

I am life, and I am peace, I am liberty; I am truth, I am love, I am the
21st Century
Life is too short for doubt, for my words to be sad, so I reach from
within, where my heart is glad

My soul breathes warmth and passion, my spirit is always on high
Everywhere I turn is God's love, and that will not pass me by

Life as we know it, will come to an end
But how many truly believe, that Jesus is there as our friend

As my soul reaches out to Thee, so will time; as it claims your heart, as
well as mine

Happy, and free, not otherwise, it shapes and moves, reality's pride

Knowing that God's word, does breathe life
Eyes will be open, and a new day will be adorned

Be free of things that you cannot change, and be mindful of the things
that you can

Live like your life was meant for you
Stay positive, trust in God, and believe in yourself

The Autumn Breeze

That day, I felt nature
As I absorbed the autumn breeze

Cultivated by the colors
Of the falling leaves

All around me, was orange, yellow, and red
A picture perfect rainbow, stretched out over my head

I could feel God's presence, with Him watching over me
As the leaves fell from the sky

Out of the autumn trees

Why can't man see the beauty of what I see
Nature calling for all of us to be real and be free

As the fall breeze turns, and makes way across the land
My emotions run deep within me as a man

Sharing God's presence really made me feel alive
As it took away my pity and it opened up my eyes

There I was in Heaven, tending to His garden
When I looked up during the autumn breeze and found favor, in His
Son, Jesus Christ

The Beauty of Christmas

It all started, with a baby in a manger
Wise men and angels
Frankincense, myrrh and gold
The King of kings, the Savior's birth

This is, one of those special times of the year
When our living spirit
Breathes Christmas cheer

The traditional snows, crystal flakes
All of this brings peace, to our hearts
As our souls awake

Christmas, joy, to every, girl and boy
As, silent kisses fall
And up comes, gifts and toys

The beauty of Christmas, the love of life
The thrill of victory, Jesus Christ

He bared our sins, when he died for us on that cross
Now Christmas cheer
Is embraced, by all at no cost

Tears of joy, love, and rest
Peace on earth and happiness

The Center of My Soul

Jesus, you are the center of my soul
And there is so much more that I, need to know

I am blessed, with your perfection, guided, by your direction
Jesus, you are my truth that must be told

I marvel at the blessings, that you lay down at my feet
I marvel about this life in me, that I know is so unique
But most of all, I marvel, at how you guided my hand
Jesus, you are the center, of this man
Jesus you matched me, with a kind and kindred soul When I thought
that I had been passed over, but little did I know

You blessed me with this angel, that I know is your Christian child
As I marvel on my knees, she looks at me and then she smiles
Jesus you're the center of my soul

Jesus in you, I know there is nothing lost
And every time I lose my way, my doubt and my belief, pay the cost

So I pray, with much conviction, that my heart knows
Jesus, above all else, you're the center of my soul

The City of Joy

There is Joy in this City, in this City, of yours and mine
There is peace, as much peace, that we will ever find

There is hope, unspeakable hope, hope that won't turn her back
Look within yourself, and see the truth from where you're at

You might be hurting, because this physical life, is real
But in the City of Joy, all suffering and pain will heal

You might be up, some things may get you down
You are looking for a City, that you know is Heaven bound

The City of Joy is offered, and the Spirit hears your plea
Open up your eyes, and your Heart will be set free

Look at me Brother, I am here to let you know
That the City of Joy, should light up that peace running in your soul

Life, is born, and death, is at our door
Never take for granted, what you've been looking for

Turn, it over, be healed and be free
Because the City of Joy, is lit up for you and me

I am, going to charge you, because, I know you hear
Stand up, for your City, you have nothing to fear

The Creator of the Universe

In my writings it's not often, that I hit a wall
As I gather up my information, I can't, seem to tell it all

This week was a challenge, but I was so inspired
I learned so much about myself, that it had my soul on fire

As I look back at this world, as openly as I can
There has been so much accomplished, and still so much more, that I
can do as a man

All History is important; all cultures are meaningful in life
God is the creator of all; it is all that He has sacrificed

He sent us His only Son Jesus, then we nailed Him to the cross
He bled and He died, so that not one of His souls, would be lost

We all probably have, a few stories that we can tell
Even if those stories, didn't turn out well

But I know for myself, the chain of command, and it starts and it ends
With Jesus' outstretched hands

He wants to lead us and guide us, along the way, and He wants to share
with us
The promise, of a better day

All of History is important, and History will not rest
Until we look to Jesus, who will always offer up His best

He is the creator of the Universe; He is the creator of all man
He is Immanuel and, He is, The Great I Am

Concepción Volcano
Ometepe Island, Nicaragua

The Clock's Running Down

The clock's running down, I hear, and everybody's laying low
No one can hide, when time expires, we got to go

We've all made bad choices, throughout, and along the way
We took the wrong turn, when we thought it was okay

A wasted life, gone down the drain, when it could have been saved, in Jesus' name

God is Alpha, and Omega, my friend, He blew life in our soul, and He knew when it would end

The clock's running down, and it's perfectly clear
Confess with your mouth, you'll have nothing to fear

Your heart must change, so the truth can be known
Christ is God, and He is God alone

The Face of Hope

When you see me, and I have seen you
There is a sense of hope, that is set and true

We believe in the preservation of life
We believe in the Father, the Son, Jesus Christ

We have been put down, far too long
We are starting to believe again, that we are not our own

Whatever wrong, that you have done
Just remember that, you are still God's son

Whoever tried to tell you, that you couldn't cope
They are liars, and you are, the face of hope

Hope had to have had, a beginning
This hope that we are living today, is not our end

Look around you, people, hope is everywhere that life begins

We are that hope, Christ died on that cross
So who here can say, that they are lost

With ministers, prophets, evangelists and friends
There is not a better people, that would see you to the end

Nothing comes easy, and we should all know that
So live life to the fullest, with God intact

The face of hope is alive
So release your fears, and open up your eyes

The Father of Light

In this world I have died daily, so many times before
But in today's dying, resurrection has been assured

I am comforted, by the sweet knowing of my soul, as my heart dances
Counting its blessings, as they unfold

Here I am, Lord, in the light, please send me
As every fiber of my being, molded into the image of your perfection
Has been loosed, has been set free

My ears hear, my heart knows the way
As I walk therein knowing, that I am that light that touches every day

Every good gift, lies in man, who has been shaped, molded, and crafted
According to the Master's plan

As I slept, I was awakened, I felt His warmth, I felt His healing

That light, that passed through my understanding
Was the Father, was me, still me, and forever

The Heart of Welch

Fridays at the Park, are going to blow your mind
At high noon, we're going to have a good time
Check out the mural, painted on that wall, Tom Acosta's talents just tell
it all
We're at Martha Moore's Park, where her legacy rests
Our job here today, is to give you our best

We're here to share music, and we know you will have some fun
While you eat at your leisure, as you're basking in the sun
Maybe you'll take a dip, in Linkus Park swimming pool
Swim enough laps, you might even stay cool

I'm the G-Man and I'm here to say, welcome everybody, to Welch's in
the Park, Fridays
Drop your guard, and ease your mind, we're not here to get fresh, but to
have a good time,
Clap your hands, or stomp your feet, listen to your heart, you'll get the
right beat,

We're McDowell County, so open up your eyes, the love you'll feel, will
be no surprise A shout out to the Mayor, and to all of my friends
Ya'll stay cool, let the entertainment begin

The Keeper of the House

I have vowed to keep the house
Winter, summer, spring, or fall

I have vowed to keep one thought
Positive and pure

I have vowed with my mind and soul
To caretake and never fold

This you get from me
As I strive to oversee

Grass grows out, dust settles in
I'm the keeper of the house
In the lion's den

Noble, to just one thought
Positive and pure

A place, where I can go
Inwardly secure

The New Generation

Are we talking about this country or are we talking about our life
Are we talking about our Creator, or man's opinion or his advice

Is this new generation, up to the task, or will they mimic their leaders, as
they hide their faces behind masks

God is real, no matter how many times you think life disappoints you
He is the God of mercy, and His power will always heal

I consider myself to be a part of these soldiers in the Lord, and I am still
going strong, And my faith in God has heightened, His grace leads me,
on one accord

Being over fifty, has not held me back, the Bible tells me that my
spiritual truth, is whatever state I am at

I am a confident believer, in the only wise and true God, who can never
be tempted, or His faith ever be robbed

I have been fortunate, in how I have been taught, and neither has my
faith wavered or been lost
But as you very well know, every sacrifice has a cost
The new generation of faith is action to the Word
Peace and truth and a voice to be heard

The Park

Me and my dog Pepper
Rode down to the city park
He was so excited about going
That all he did was bark

He stuck his head out the truck window
To smell the spring time air
With the wind blowing
Pepper knew we were almost there

We finally made it to the park
As I set down at a nearby table to write
Pepper took off running
But never let me out of his sight

We were the only ones there that day
But it was still okay
The sun didn't shine
But me and Pepper, we had peace of mind

Pepper explored the park
And I used my time to write
Soon it'll be time to go back home
And I know that Pepper will put up a fight

Pepper is black with brown under his belly and on his paws
Part chow and the prettiest little dog you ever saw
As we started back home with the wind blowing through his hair
Pepper stood up on the arm of my seat looking back without a care

The Power of Christ

Though the clouds, try
To hide our blue, blue skies

Know that the truth, will be revealed, before
Our eyes

Though the time, seems, to have stopped
Before our lives

There is still victory in Christ
And the Son will always Rise

I know it will, I believe in Him
The truth is mine, and I am His

And if you are still doubting, and don't feel free
Then follow your heart, which beats within thee

I will pray to God, that your eyes will open up to see
As I bow my head, and fall down on my knees

He is the Christ, that's within our lives
He is our strength, no other can suffice

He is the Lord and God of all
Don't forget, that the power of Christ, cannot fall

Everything else, may contain a lie
So search for the truth and you will know why

God is our Father and we are His daughters and sons
Let peace be still, He is the One

The Promise Keeper

He is always the God of His word, what you speak to Him, is
always heard
He is the promise keeper, our God, our mission, who values life,
more than any tradition

If we don't believe in something, we will fall for anything, so I ask
you
Wouldn't you rather feel good in your spirit, and whole in your
soul
Never have to worry about looking back, or feel guilty because you
didn't follow the flow

I am worthy of His promises, I am the heir of the promise keeper, I
vow to be loyal, I vow to be true
There is nothing more important to me, than my friendship to you

The Soul of a Nation

We used to be, the strongest nation in the world
And we used to believe, that God put us there

But taking prayer, out of our schools
Has me wondering, if any one of us still care

We are a country, of many faces
We are the land, of the free

We are the soul of a nation, her freedom lies
Within, you and me

Our structure is firm, God's truth becomes our strength
And the reality that sustains us, is something we won't resent

Misunderstood and misrepresented, we are still shackled in chains

We are the soul of our nation, but no one remembers our name

History is made, change has come
The era of a generation, has brought new life back to the Son

The Spirit of Christmas

Who determines the Spirit of Christmas
Will our soul be okay?

Are we teaching the birth of Jesus
Or forsaking the blessings that come our way

Have we really been thankful
For the things that He has done

Have we looked back over our lives
And just labeled Him as God's forgotten Son

Have we dotted all of our I's
Have we crossed all of our T's

In the spirit of Christmas
Have we dropped down on our knees

Are we consumed by tradition
Has it taken away the joy

Knowing that Christ was born, will we let
His spirit in us be destroyed

This day is eventful
It has spread a lot of love

Love that has a new beginning
Starting with every person that we think of

But who determines the Spirit of Christmas
Will it come and go without a trace

When we look in the mirror
Will we see mercy and grace, or just another image
Of our own selfish face.

The Still Waters

As I stand here beside the still waters, as I reflect back on the blessings of my life
I am moved in my spirit, and by the presence of Jesus Christ

Yesterday, I was an infant, cradled in my Mama's arms
I was safe, and secure, not exposed and not alarmed

But today, I stand with Mother's nature, as like a butterfly that shall spread her wings
Lifting, my praises higher, as the truth of life, begins to swing

This is that revealing moment, that has defined just who I am
Thank you Lord for your promises, which I know will never let me down

I have expanded my vision, that I have kept along the way

And I am saved through grace, as mercy follows me each day

The still waters of my being, have become the still waters of my life

I am content in knowing, that my heart belongs to Christ

The Sunflower

I grew a sunflower
That stood as tall as a tower

Its leaves were as wide as the day
And when it opened up
Its beauty smiled at the high heavens

Some talked about it
As if they could read its mind
As it shined
Beautifully

I am ever so proud
Because that sunflower stood yellow and loud

It had a message that everyone knew
Oh, how that sunflower grew

The ants, and the bugs
Also celebrated

As the sunflower grew
They feasted

Carving their marks in the bark
Of its being

Not too many can say, that they grew a sunflower

That shined as bright as the day
That turned heads, when people came its way

That also was a bed, which fed
God's creation

The True Legacy of an Icon

My Dad knows his destiny, and so should we, this legacy of an Icon, is the spiritual blessing that you see

My Dad is blessed, throughout the ages of time
A man who is no stranger, but who is always your friend and mine

Words won't describe, all of the good, that he does
But all of us have been touched, by the legacy of his love

He means so much, to so many, as his worth will live on
His body may be getting older, but his spirit, is alive and strong

He gives so much, and asks for so little in return
A man who is more, than the credit that he has earned

The road that he travels, always represents the right foundation of God
And the truth that he stands for, is always challenged but never robbed

This is the legacy of an Icon, and I am the vision that he saw
Every success that I have achieved, comes from God's Son, who has no flaw

The Typewriter Blues – I Won't Shine No Shoes

For so very long, I have waited patiently for you
To get my hands on you so that you could say my name
I am in a dream world and I know you feel the same
We are different but I have never seen a more equal match
Look how we latch
I can hold my head high, now, knowing that you care
Knowing that I turn you on and knowing that
You will always be there
Some might think it strange that I feel this way
But listening to you, lets me know that
It's going to be okay
You don't doubt me, you just go along
You share my feelings even if they are wrong
The moment I saw you, it blessed my heart
Deep down where the rivers never part
I had struck out so many times before
But not no more
And you will always be, the one that I adore
As my fingers run across your divine
My sole purpose is not to leave your feelings behind
But to cherish this moment that I know is mine.
I won't shine no shoes

There is a God

Never mind what others have told you
Look within yourself

Believe within your consciousness
That throughout this confusion, something good is still left

Concerning the things that we were taught
It was the information that we had

But you know within your heart
That you can change it, if it's bad

There is a God, who sets up high and looks down low
Who will always be there, to bless our mortal soul

God is truly, a good friend of mine
The world has been unfair, but His love is always on time

There has been this unveiling life
And the truth that exists, lies within our understanding of Jesus Christ

All that we would like to see, and all that we would want to be
Is stored up in a safe place, inside of you and me

There is a Savior, and I know that He is real
It is not what I can see, but how it is, that He makes me feel

There is No Shame in Rejoicing

Who is this versatile spirit, that stands before the King
Confessing and believing, that God is their everything

Who is this versatile spirit, that bows down to pray
Who never doubts for a moment, that the Lord will make a way

There is no shame in rejoicing, there is no shame in God
The author and the finisher of our faith, that cannot be robbed

Nothing does come easy, and humbleness reaps its reward
There is no shame in stepping out, because the world in its state, is hard

Rejoicing makes you feel better, rejoicing makes you feel alive
The only death that we will ever see, is when the old man surrenders in
us and dies

Don't be a pretender, God already knows our hearts
Drop on our knees and confess with our mouth
Our love for Jesus is a start

We rejoice because we can, always give the Lord some praise
We are dead to this world, but the new man in us has been raised

Things Learned But Never Forgotten

I can smile with you, and we can talk
We can share secrets, and we can walk...together

Even though it is our choice, to be friends
The world looks down on us, as though it is our end

Things that are learned, hatred that is never forgotten
Makes this sad in a day

The hurt and the pain that one endures, may never be seen
But it is never forgotten

Stating that life once lived with its riches and gold
Can sometimes be so rotten

But truth will rise to tell it all
Love will always hear her call

This Blessed Thanksgiving

AND LAST NIGHT'S PUMPKIN PIE

It's so good to be alive, and so good to be in this right frame of mind
So good to see my mother-in-law this morning
Thank God this, blessed Thanksgiving is yours and mine

It was so good, to talk to my mother and father on the phone
Even though I am miles, and miles away from home

It is so good to have my wife, close, and to hold her in my arms
To assure her of my love for her, this blessed Thanksgiving morn

It is so good to know that Sarah, and Leah, are in Jesus' hands
So good to thank God for a cousin, who is responding to His command

It is surely a blessed Thanksgiving morning, to reach out to family and friends
To share a purpose in this day, asking God for forgiveness for our sins

It's a blessed Thanksgiving morning, to watch my wife and mother-in-law
Prepare our Thanksgiving feast
To know that the love that they have put into it, will be such a wonderful treat

It is a blessed Thanksgiving morning, and let's not forget the Macy's Day Parade and the animals, Thumper and General Chardonnay
A blessed morning, followed by a beautiful day, with hearts of gold and love showing it God's way

This Old House

We live in a world of hope and pain, some rise up, others lose everything
It's a bitter taste, all about the mouth, and all that we have believed in, turns into a sea of doubt
God cares, who lives or dies, but we can see hope fading, before our eyes
Sooner or later, it's going to take its toll, we are the walking dead, with no comfort to our soul
Lost in a world, with no relief, the sun going down, as darkness creeps
Tear-drops falling, time's running out, why should I worry, leaving this world in doubt? Then God whispers softly, in my ear, "Close your eyes child, there is nothing to fear."
"Come on home, you'll be okay, this old house that is falling, it was made of clay
Its structure filled your life, with mercy and grace, and it gave you power, to run this race, now, all that you have lost, I will soon replace."
"Lay down your burdens, and follow Me, your spirit is not dead, but your soul is free."
"All is well, in this house of Mine, the mansion I built, will stand throughout the hands of time."
"Stretch out your arms, your faith is healed, walk in the light, My word is for real."
In this old house, where there was pain, and the pain did not cease
God said to be still, God is truth, and truth is peace

Thunder

As I look into this mirror, my mind is so blind
It sees, it understands, but still it finds no time

Is it any wonder, what those thoughts are under
Stuck there between the tracks, wondering how to make it back

I know that there is no innocence, in the way that we think
And I know that my own thoughts, sometimes may stink

I know that this world has manipulated, the good intentions of our heart
Our flames burn so low that the wick don't spark

But I also know that God has the gift of life, as we live in His paradise
Stretched between these tracks, trying to make it back

II Corinthians ten and four, tells me that God's warfare is not carnal
That I must be 100% sure in my belief or continue suffering in doubt
and grief

So that when I look into the mirror,
I am convinced of what I see
Genesis four and seven, staring back at me

I might have been on thunder road,
But God's grace and mercy, has blessed my soul.

Trickled Down

Our aim is life, and our objective, is Christ

These are our perilous times, and without the faith of a savior
Your world ends, and so does mine

There is no power on this Earth, that is greater than that of Christ
And as the old man dies in us daily, he awakens to a new life

We are blessed beyond measures, but often we forget
That the God of our Creation, is not done with us yet

We blocked out the fears, that had us in tears
But it is God who has healed Us, it is God who makes things clear
God made us this promise, and I know that He cares

He wants us inspired, like Moses
He wants us hungry, like Paul
He wants us able to accomplish our goals, when we think that we have
lost sight of them all

Time has trickled down on man, in a world that has gone cold
And the angels are taking back the spirits, of the young and old

The road that we have traveled, has become swift and clear
And we know that perilous times for man, in this world are finally here

God's perfect world where man's pleasure, has been measured by his
riches and gold
God's world where man's lust of his eyes, has lost man his eternal soul

There is a reason to worry, so we must believe
Our aim is life, our objective is Christ, Christian don't be deceived

Virginia

I am so passionate about so many things, I am so moved by what's in a
name
Virginia, they told me you were my enemy, they told me that the war
would live on
What they forgot to tell me, was that true love could right any wrong
No matter the situation, we don't ever have to be alone

Virginia, whatever history has been made by you in the past
Has nothing to do with me but my history with you will last

I am still loyal to West Virginia, because it is still my home
Where heavens in the mountains tell me, almost Heaven is where I
belong

Virginia, I see you different now, I see the love that you have shown
You touched me in so many ways, which will keep our feelings going on

I've also seen your beauty, I've seen nature at its best
I've seen so much good in you, that it's put my soul to rest

Will I tell others about the way, you have made me feel
Will I write a melody about the Virginia, I'm beginning to know so well

Maybe I can tell them about the love of my life, that started when a girl
named Sarah
Gave me some good advice

Maybe I can tell them about the woman of my dreams, that said yes
Then the wind stood still, as I put on my Sunday's best

Virginia, I am passionate about so many things, but what I am more
passionate about
Is learning what's in a name

Waiting on the Bus

I asked a lady the other day, if she needed a ride
Thirty miles from Welch, we were, but she could not
decide

I smiled, and then, I asked her again
She smiled back, with bus fare in her hand

She politely declined, the reason was clear, in my rearview mirror, the
bus was here

I wasn't shocked, people do this sort of thing, all of the
time
They've gotten so comfortable, that they take the bus up
and down this line

She was not a stranger, but God knew best
Leaving her behind, my soul was at rest

The wind blowing, mildly, in my face
I got back on 52, and continued on my pace

I felt the presence of God, who assures me
My heart races to the tune, as He secures me

A successful morning, a beautiful day
With the arm of the Lord around me, life is okay

Walking the Walk

Some people, just like to talk the talk, and there are others who truly,
walk the walk

As enthusiastically as I prepare to live,
I am convinced that the efforts of my preparation, clear my mind
It often takes me back to a place, where purity, is all I find

I am reminded of all that is good, that still exists in the hearts of man
As my Comforter gently shares those feelings, and then He reaches
down, and touches my hand

Living is for everybody, and living is a state of mind
Do what you will, with your life
But your heart says, it must beat on time

I know that in living life, I am doing the best I can and I know that
God keeps my body safe
I've also looked back over my life
And I know that it was God's love, that gave me this grace

I can talk the talk, and I can also, walk the walk
Keep your heart beating with the pace
It makes a difference, in this life that you face

We Have Been Served

Like a thief in the night, He will come again
And the truth will reveal itself, throughout the land

Steady your lives, because you have been served
Trust and believe, and we will get what we deserve

Day after day, He has shown us the way
And the word that has been preached, is Heaven which is here to stay

We must cast all of our cares, if we dare
God is present, so we better be aware

We have been served, we must ease our minds
Live like our hearts, are one of a kind

We must pray to the Father, and give honor to the Son
And remember in truth, that our time has come

We must hold onto this gift, of eternal life
We have been served, so we must keep it right

The Son of Man, is Jesus Christ
And our anointed walk, should always be in the light

Well Wishing

People search up and the people search down
Looking for that wonderful place, that will never be found

Turning to their own understanding, and finding none
Not being humble enough to know where they have come from

Let me tell you something and this I know
Peace can be found, but it is not in your ego

God will give you wishes and the best in life
But we must first acknowledge, that He is God and Jesus Christ

We can live forever, in a land that has no peace
Where well-wishing will come together, but truth in God will never cease

We can go to our Daddy, who's in Heaven, and who is our friend
And He will give us peace everlasting, that will never end

Well-wishing is fine, but you really ought to know
Sooner or later, you will have to choose which way you're going to go

God will comfort you, He will wrap you in His arms
Make you a believer, and keep you safe, from danger and harm

Well-wishing in this world, can be a dead end street
But if you're soul searching, well-wishing in Jesus, He will be there to give you peace

When Death Came Knocking

When death came knocking, like it had before, some still were doing less, and others were still doing more

It is the last hurdle that we have to overcome, to live with the Father, and rest with the Son

We have to be sure of the life that we have led, and be ready to see Heaven, after we have made our bed

I saw myself deep in the Master's arms, so when death came knocking, I was not alarmed

I knew the truth, and it set me free
Because the faith that I felt, was not only for my eyes to see
But it was the substance of that, which certainly set me free

When fear came knocking, God opened the door
And it was His peace, that came rushing, like never before

God held my hand, and He brought me through
Death is always searching, for me and you
Tears of joy, are always there to soothe our soul
When our loved ones pass, through the valley, of the dark, dead and cold

It is then, when our tears, are finally made clear
When the still, small voice tells us, that there is nothing to fear

When is Enough, Enough?

We have climbed into the 21st century
But tell me, what has changed

The faces are different, but the players, remain the same

Unless you have some experience, of what I am talking about
You will always be, dragging your feet, through a cloud of doubt

Justice is sometimes unfair, and life keeps us on the run
But one thing is for sure, with God, we are never done

If there has never been an occasion, where intolerance has happened to
you
You will have no idea, about what the rest of us, are going through

When is enough, enough? When there is a change?
And how can we feel good about America?
When everything, remains the same

Death is not the only component, that keeps our life in fear
It is a moment like this when we gather
And learn that we must dry up our tears

I have made up my mind, and enough, is enough
Things are still not equal and times are still tough

But I have turned it over, and it is in God's care
If you are really serious, about issues
Let God make it right for you, out there

When will enough be enough?

When it Rains, How Do You Feel

I sit at my dining room table, when I am able, it is raining, I listen to it fall
I hear the morning birds singing, and the sounds, just tell it all

When I think about the rain, and how it falls, when Jesus calls
I am blessed beyond measure, because I am a witness to it all

This is how I feel when the skies open up, and life takes a drink
That beautiful sound of the rain, makes me stop and think

Here is Heaven, pouring down her blessings, that so many try to deny
Like the sound of one's heart that beats, the truth has to open up her eyes

God set this table, and then He covered it with a cloth,
Then the rain came pouring down, and Mother's Nature wasn't lost

When it rains, how do you feel?
Sitting at this table, when I able, I am blessed, and it is real.

Who Am I

At times, I wonder
Who am I

Trying not, to live a lie
But live eternally, till the day I die

Still my heart pants
Searching for a reason

Torn between the seasons

Who am I

So many years have gone by
Often so hard, do I try

Still sometimes
I don't know why

When I look in the mirror
Am I living a lie

Please tell me
Who am I

Am I still your little boy
Filled with love, full of joy

Am I, still your son
I know, there is still a race to run

Trying not to live a lie
Can you see the love of Jesus in my eye

Lord I am, Lord I try
But still, Lord
Who am I?

Who Told You That

A lot of times we give up, on the things that mean the most
Because someone told us that we were not worthy, we also give up on the
Holy Ghost

But who told you that you were naked, and who told you, that you were
no good
Who told you, that the price wasn't paid, because Jesus told you, that
you could
We rely so much on others, to be the caretakers of our soul
When in reality, they are the heart breakers
With no life of their own, or no goals

Who told you, that you were not wonderfully made
Who told you, that you could not be

Satan is a liar, don't let your heart be deceived

Once I was told, that I would fail
I was even told, that I was bound, for hell

But God has the devil, under His feet,
We are beautifully made, and our souls He does keep
The things of this world, have little gain
Even though we don't set out to be in vain

I have always been blessed, and that's a fact
I am that I am, it was God that told me that

Will I Ever See

My subconscious is telling me
That it will be okay

My heart is telling me
That the Lord will make a way

My conscious mind is telling me
That God always seems to be right on time

I am hoping to see things that are real
But will my heart ever see, just what it finds

I have been blinded by so many rights, knowing
That the truth in me , carries its own light

I am sure of what to do
So I'll just carry these feeling, just like you

You Are Released, from Your Fears

Love your neighbor, because God said so, search your whole heart,
And watch it grow
You are released from your fears, forget about all of the pain, that you
endured
Throughout the years, wipe your eyes, and dry your tears

Peace is waiting, fall in the open arms of God
The love of the Father, cannot be robbed

Be quiet, and then be still
Blessed is how, He will make you feel
You will be attacked, but love anyway
Turn it over to God, He will show you a better day

You Can Survive

So much has been said, about cancer, but cancer is no joke
Families have been torn apart, because in the end, they couldn't cope

Dead is real, and it's certainly not a game, the spirit of God will heal,
Any life that cancer tries to claim

My brothers and my sisters, there is a better way, Jesus said, just believe
And things will be okay

You can survive, this threat that holds you down, Jesus is the answer
To any problem that comes around
Cancer has no power, but to many it has deceived
Your joy has been taken, but stay down on your knees

Break the chains of hopelessness, sadness, and despair
Know that you are not alone, people are fighting cancer everywhere

I don't have all the answers, but I have a glimpse of what you are going
through

And I do have a friend named Jesus, who will always be there for you

Young Lovers

Some people will never understand, the time nor the day
When someone special comes along, and takes your breath away

But what God has for you, it will be for you
Keep love pure in your heart, and all of your dreams will come true

Young lovers, young friends of mine, what a life to live
During these troubled times

I saw it in your eyes, as that agape love touched me
The same way that the wind stood still, and declared my bride and me

Our love will live forever, as time passes on
And our hearts will never forget, in whom it truly belongs

Just look around, you can see how true love feels
And when you are down, you will have this image of love to heal

Some things are taken for granted
More often than we think

Keep your love fresh, and your love will never stink

Treat truth, as your breath of life, and the meditation of your heart
As the spiritual blessings of Christ

Some people have waited their entire life, for a day just like today
When someone special like you comes along, you will know it
And they will take your breath away

Your Rejoicing Spirit

Hands up to the non-profits, here in McDowell County, here's a shout-out to you

Thank you for your presence, and all of the hard work that you do

You've changed a lot of lives, and put many smiles back on our faces

God had shown you this vision, and we will try to keep up with the pace

We will never forget you, and we hope that we have touched your heart
We have much love for you, and that love will never part

Houses have been fixed, minds mended, and all is well
You've made a difference here in McDowell County
And we hope that you can tell

Your rejoicing spirit, brought back our hope
We're not fully restored, but at least now we can cope